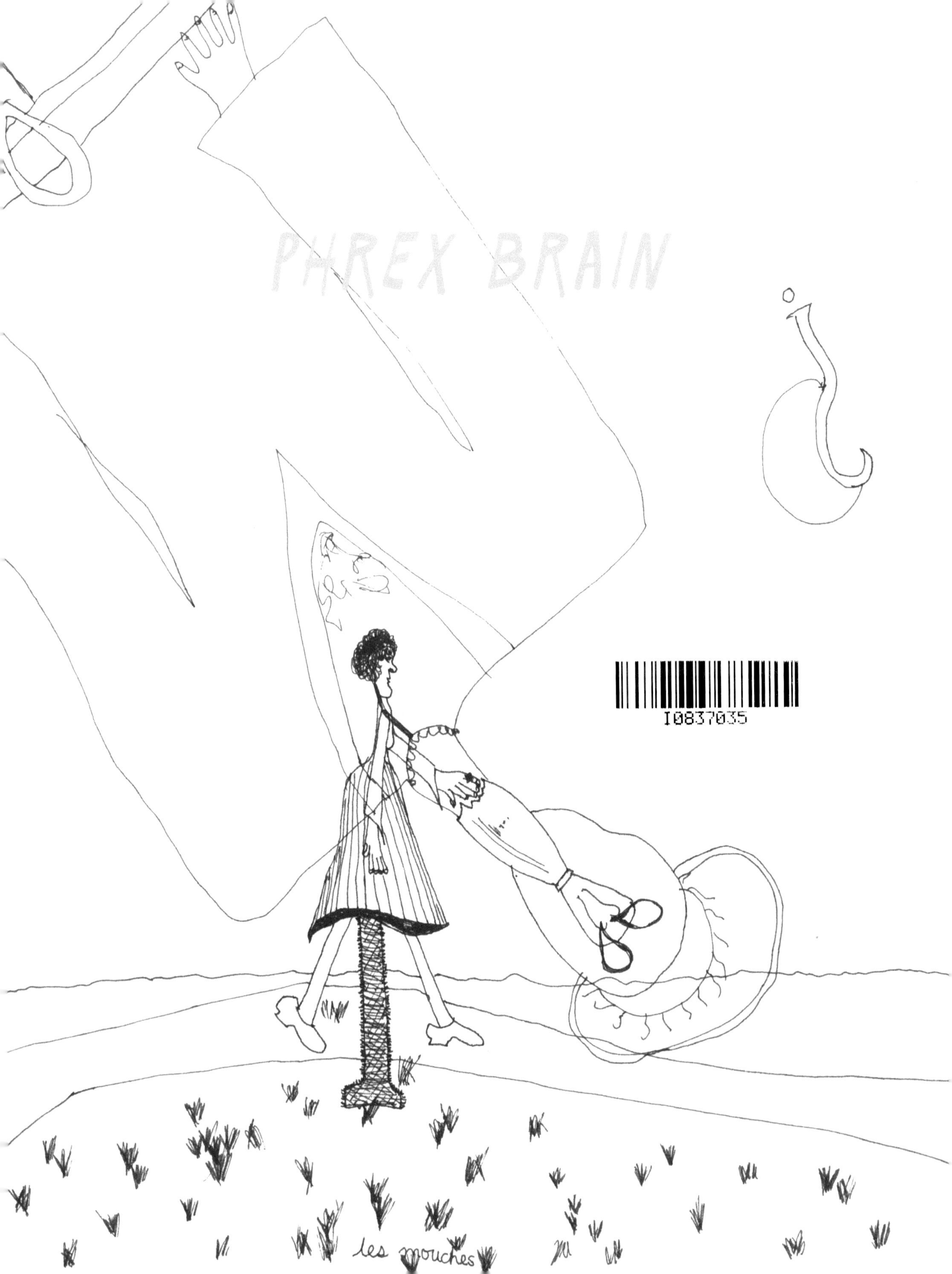
PHREX BRAIN
I0837035
les mouches

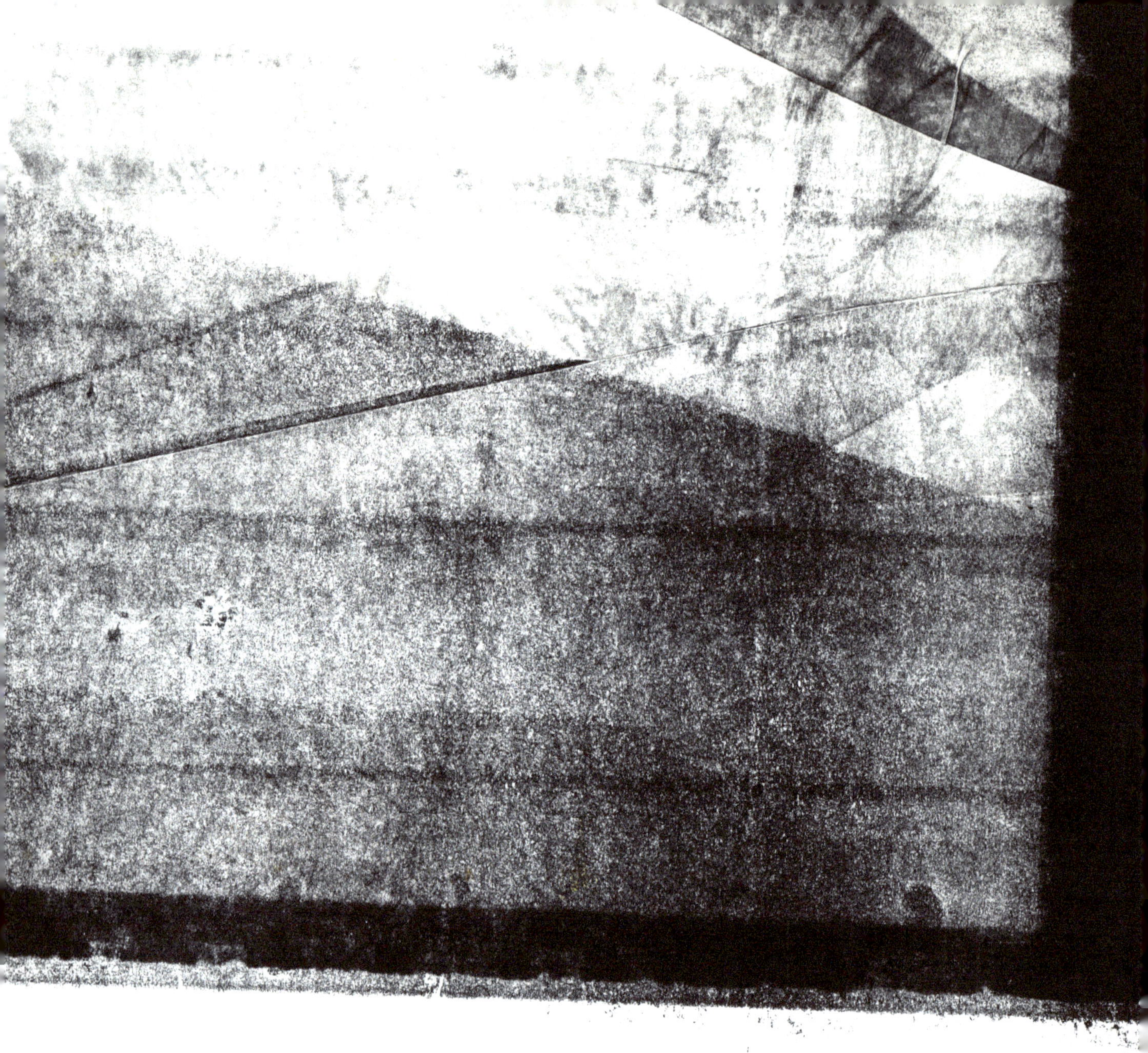

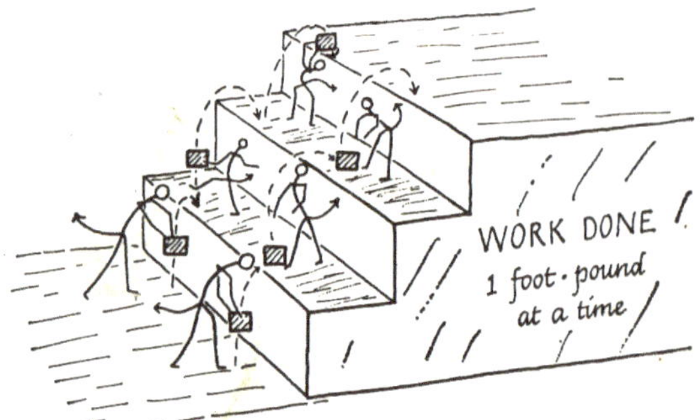

FIG. 26-4. WORK
Units demons do weight-raising job.

Some 'K'

every function

divine glad centre

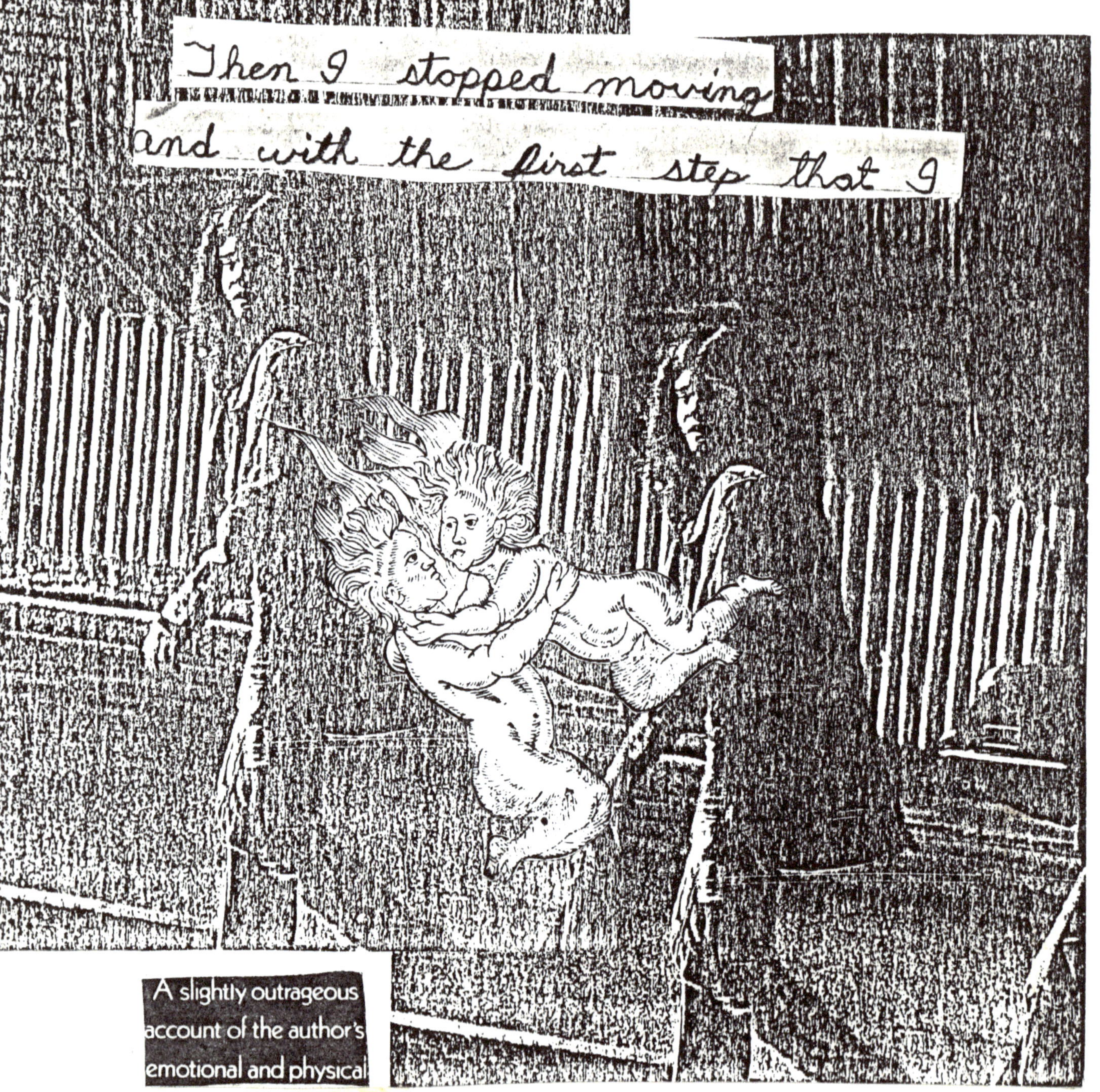

liz is

BY **elizabeth was**

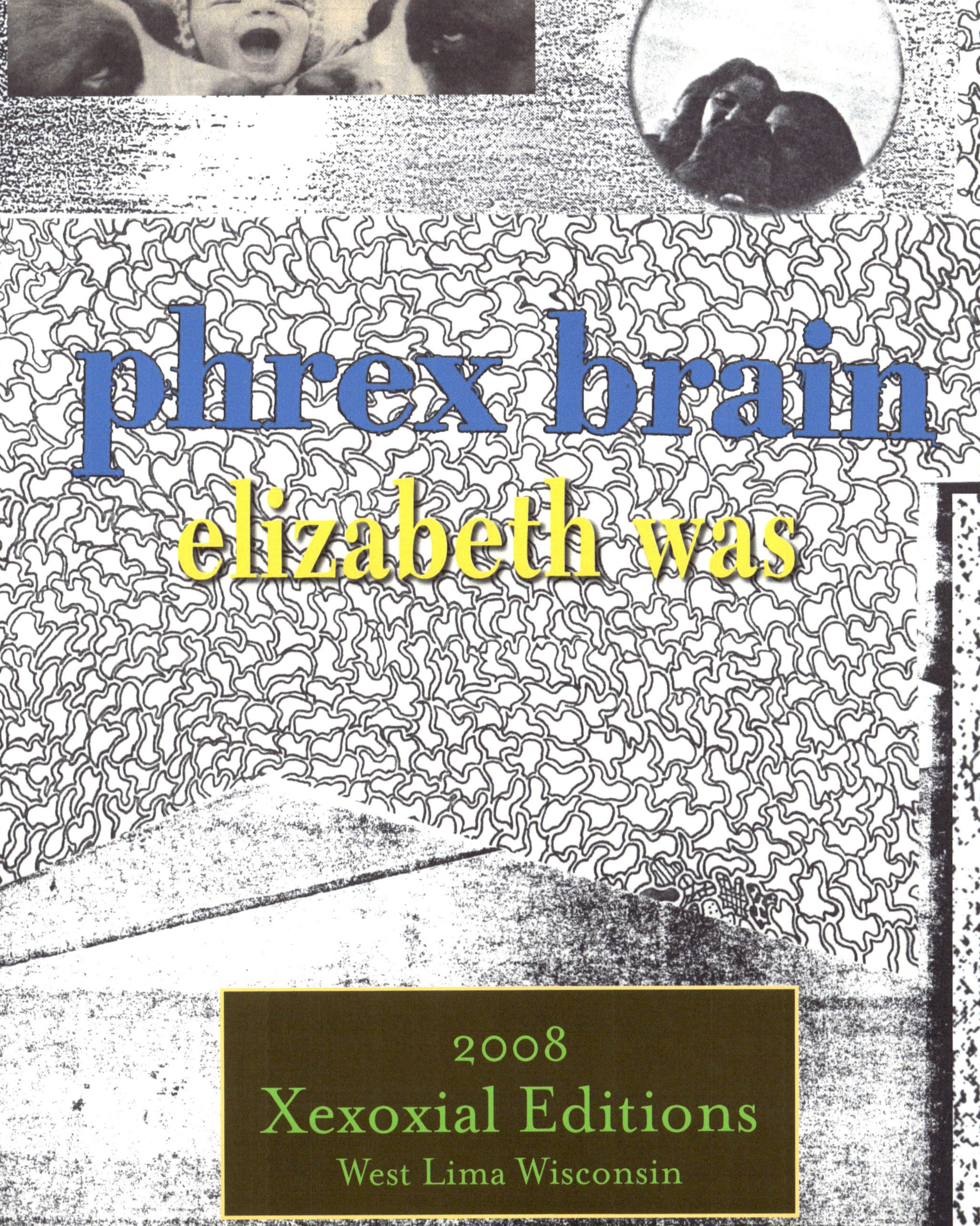

phrex brain

elizabeth was

2008
Xexoxial Editions
West Lima Wisconsin

This book was first published in 1984 by Xerox Sutra Editions.
3rd edition digitized July 2008.

ISBN-10 1-936687-16-X
ISBN-13 978-1-936687-16-9

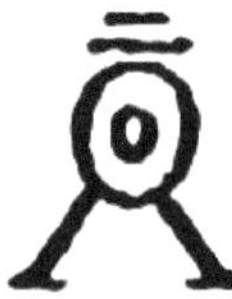

published by
Xexoxial Editions
10375 County Highway Alphabet
La Farge, WI 54639

www.xexoxial.org

perspicacity@xexoxial.org

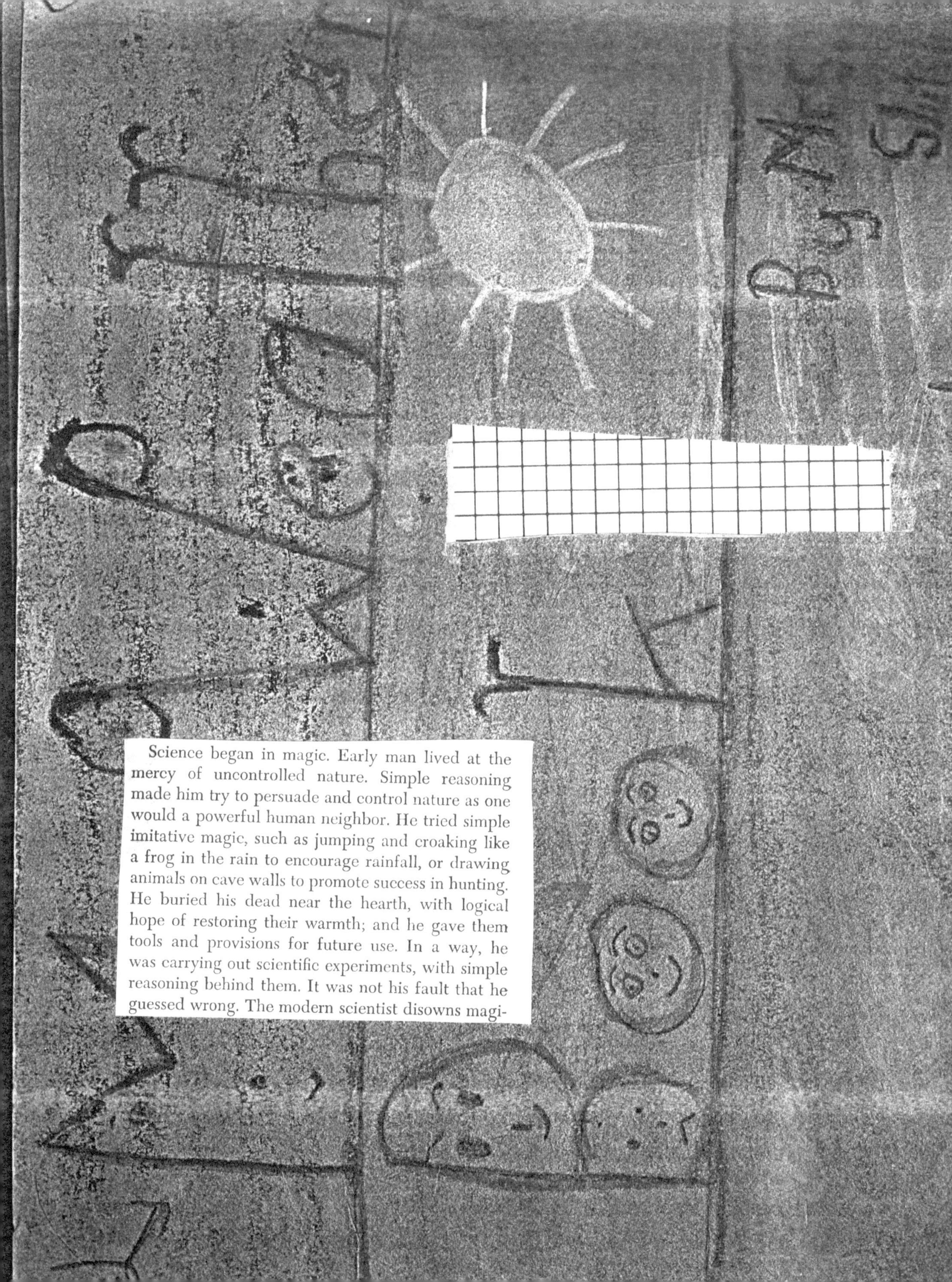

Science began in magic. Early man lived at the mercy of uncontrolled nature. Simple reasoning made him try to persuade and control nature as one would a powerful human neighbor. He tried simple imitative magic, such as jumping and croaking like a frog in the rain to encourage rainfall, or drawing animals on cave walls to promote success in hunting. He buried his dead near the hearth, with logical hope of restoring their warmth; and he gave them tools and provisions for future use. In a way, he was carrying out scientific experiments, with simple reasoning behind them. It was not his fault that he guessed wrong. The modern scientist disowns magi-

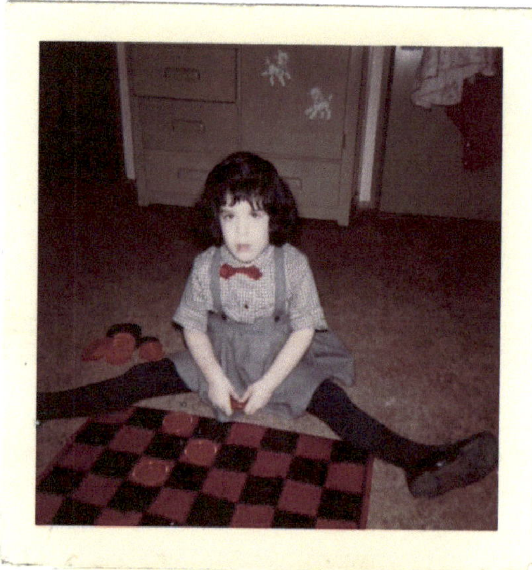

Simple Experiments with Reflection

Former literary 'also-ran' looks back on life

1.

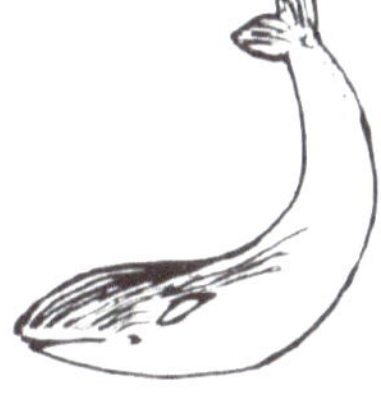

whale

Is it a __ __ ale?

Yes, it's a __ __ ale.

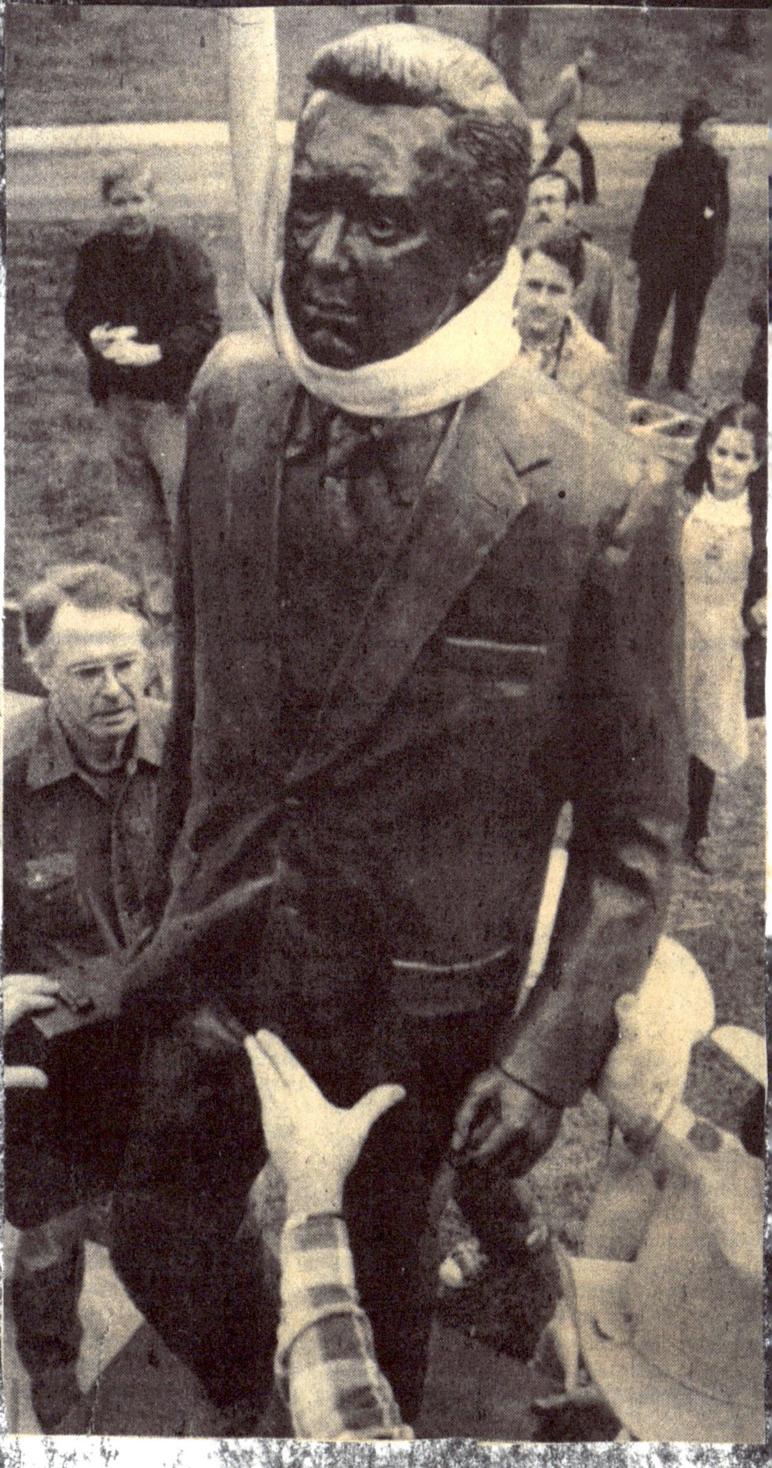

Liz Nasaw   Harbor Hill
10/24/65   Room 27

Dick Whittington and his Cat

Once there was a very poor boy, named Dick Whittington, whose parents had died when he was very young. His town in England was poor, so he didn't get much that he begged for. He had heard people talking about a wonderfully rich place called London, which was a city filled with gold and jewels. Once Dick saw a beautiful carriage riding through town. He was sure that this was from London. He asked the wagoner, (the man walking alongside the carriage) if he could walk with him. When the wagoner heard poor Dick's story his answer was yes. When they got to London, Dick was so happy, that he ran as fast as he could, and forgot to say thank-you to the kind man. A minute later, he was so tired and disappointed, because he saw no gold around, that he lay down in a dark corner and cried himself to sleep. When he woke up the next morning he was hungry and a butcher shop across the street tempted him. Dick knocked on the door

9? except neatness

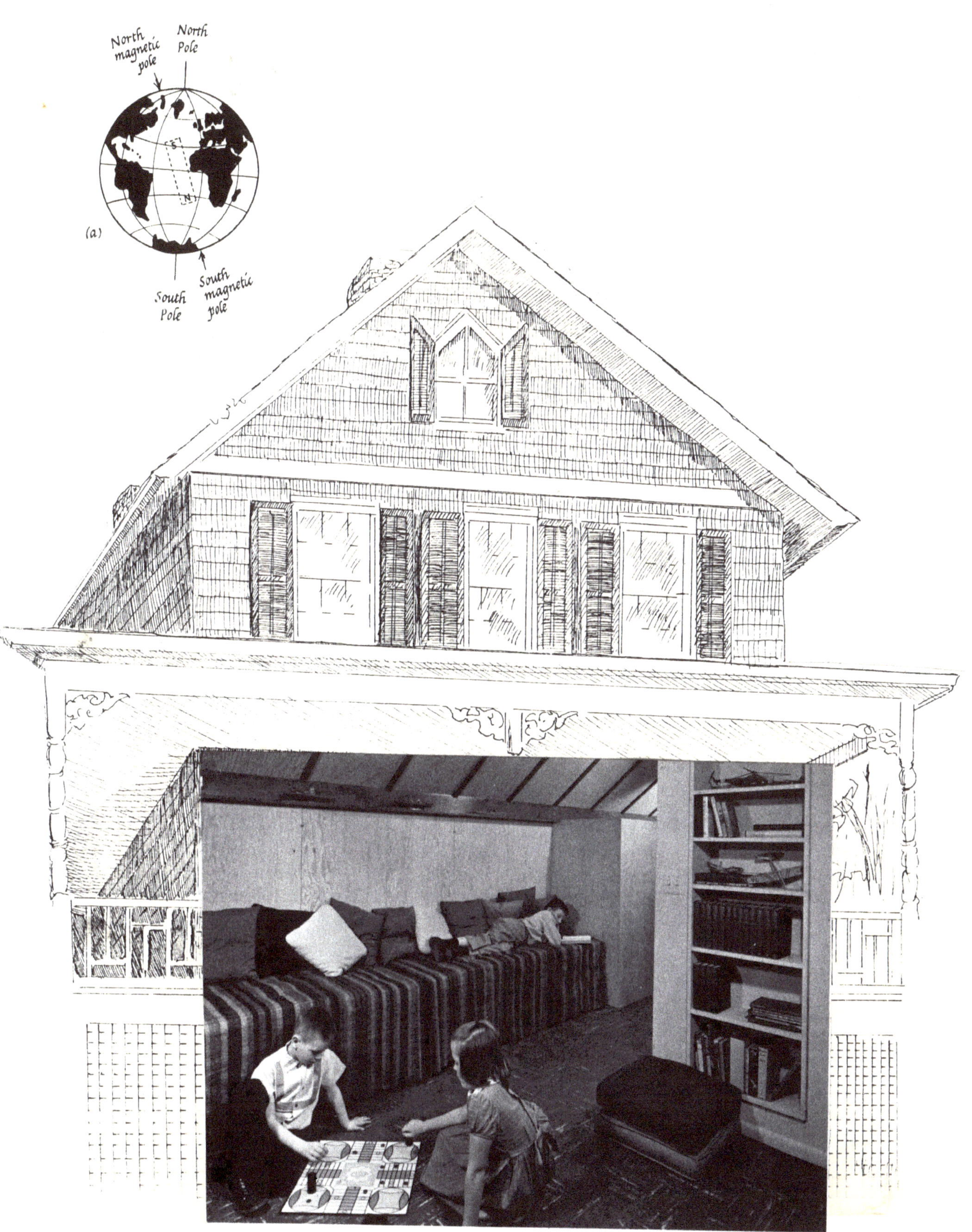

Another example of comfortable and safe play space in the finished attic. Sloped ceiling is of plywood panels. Walls have built-in storage areas for toys and personal items.

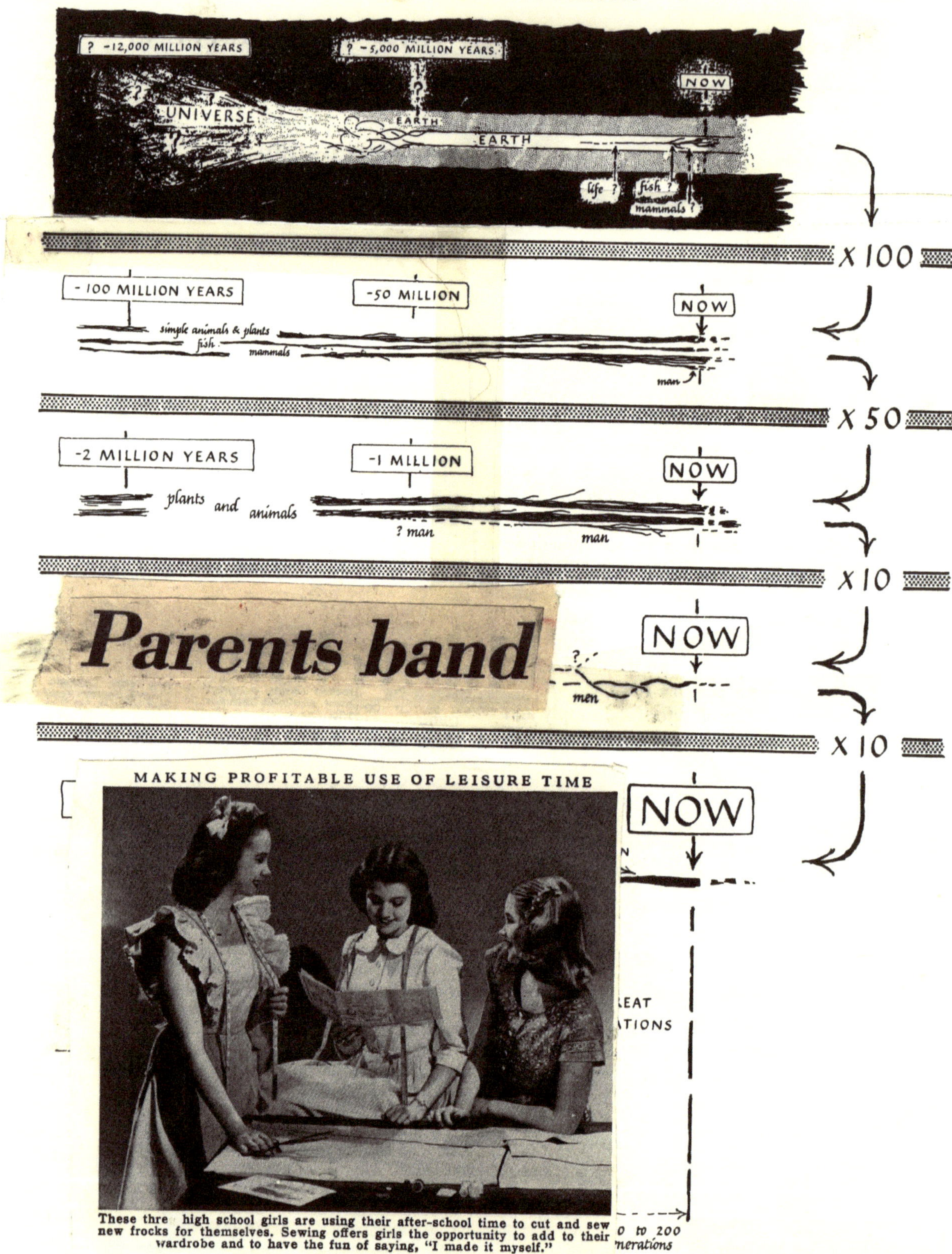

Fig. 12-1. A Rough Table of Ages

The times for the stages of man differ greatly with locality. "The age of the Universe" not only seems a fantastic guess but is also entirely dependent on our choice of time-scale: yet astrophysicists are making scientific speculations.

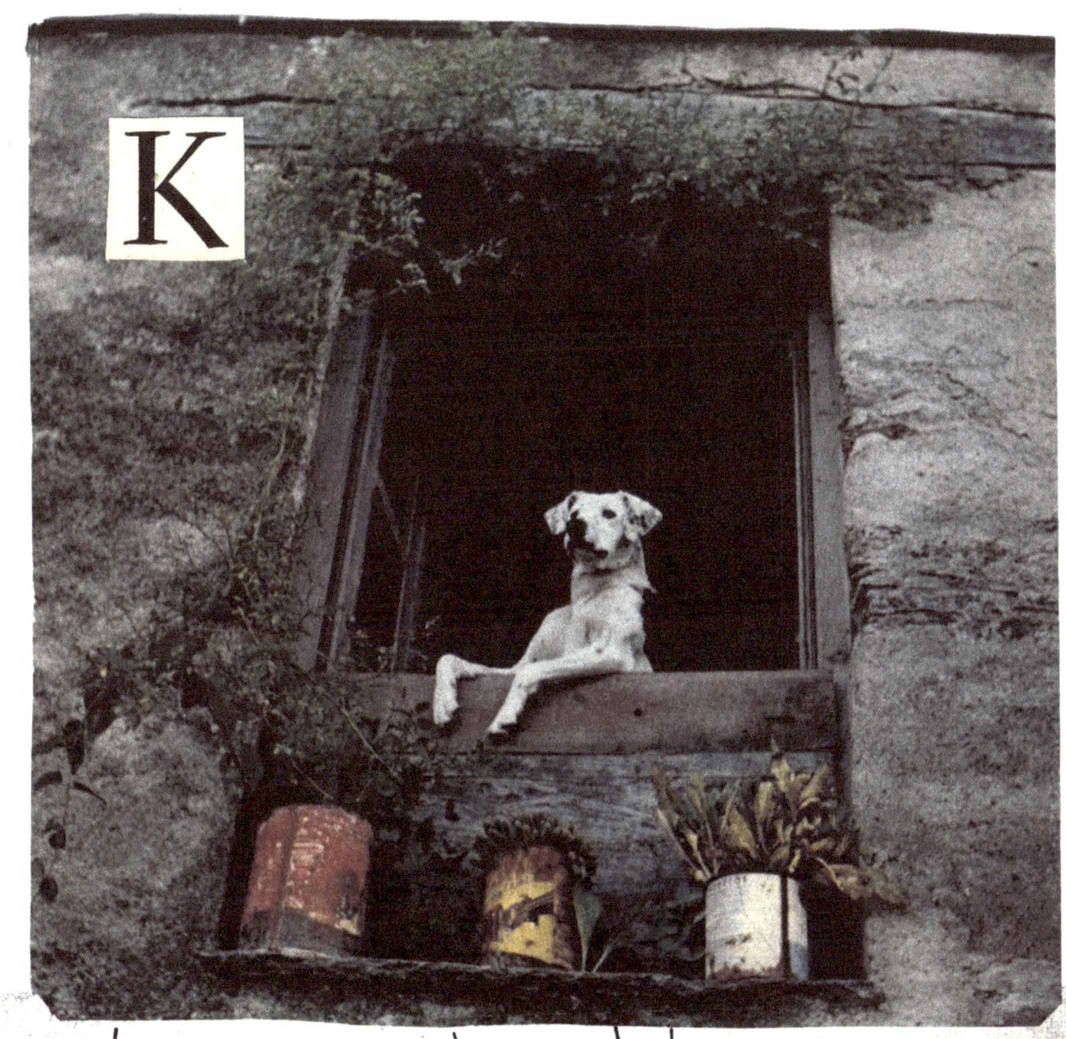

kind of shelter. Cave-
nen didn't have the things
we have now. They didn't
have electricity and lots
other things.

never came to U.S.)

5. I'm __ __ enty.

20

tr
sw
tw

6. I want __ __ies.

tr
fr
cr

1. Вѣроисповѣданіе: Іудейское

2. Время рожденія или возрастъ: Девятнадцати лѣтъ

3. Родъ занятій: приказчикъ

4. Состоитъ ли или состоялъ ли въ бракѣ: Неженатъ

5. Находится при немъ:

6. Отношеніе къ отбыванію воинской повинности:

III

Tally of people

PYGMIES

GIANTS

Cloth

При неграмотности предъявителя обозначаются его примѣты:

Ростъ: малый

Цвѣтъ волосъ: русые

Особыя примѣты: нѣтъ

Городскимъ Старостою

БЕЗПЛАТНО.
НА СРОКЪ НЕ БОЛѢЕ ОДНОГО ГОДА.

Предъявитель сего Ковенской губ., Тельшевскаго уѣзда, мѣщанинъ г. Тельшъ Бенцель Іоселевъ Кобра уволенъ въ разные города и селенія Россійской Имперіи отъ нижеписаннаго числа по 1 Апрѣля тысяча девятьсотъ пятаго года.

Дать, съ приложеніемъ печати, тысяча девятьсотъ четвертаго года Апрѣля седьмого дня.

Тельшевскій Городской Староста [signature] 2)

ОТСРОЧКА. БЕЗПЛАТНО.

Выдана Liz Nasaw *saxophone, piano* 1)

Дѣйствіе сего паспорта отсрочено на , т.-е. до года.

2)

Печать установленія, въ коемъ отсрочка выдана.

1) На пунктирѣ обозначается названіе установленія, выдавшаго паспортъ или отсрочку.
2) Пунктиръ означаетъ мѣсто для подписи лица, выдавшаго паспортъ или отсрочку.

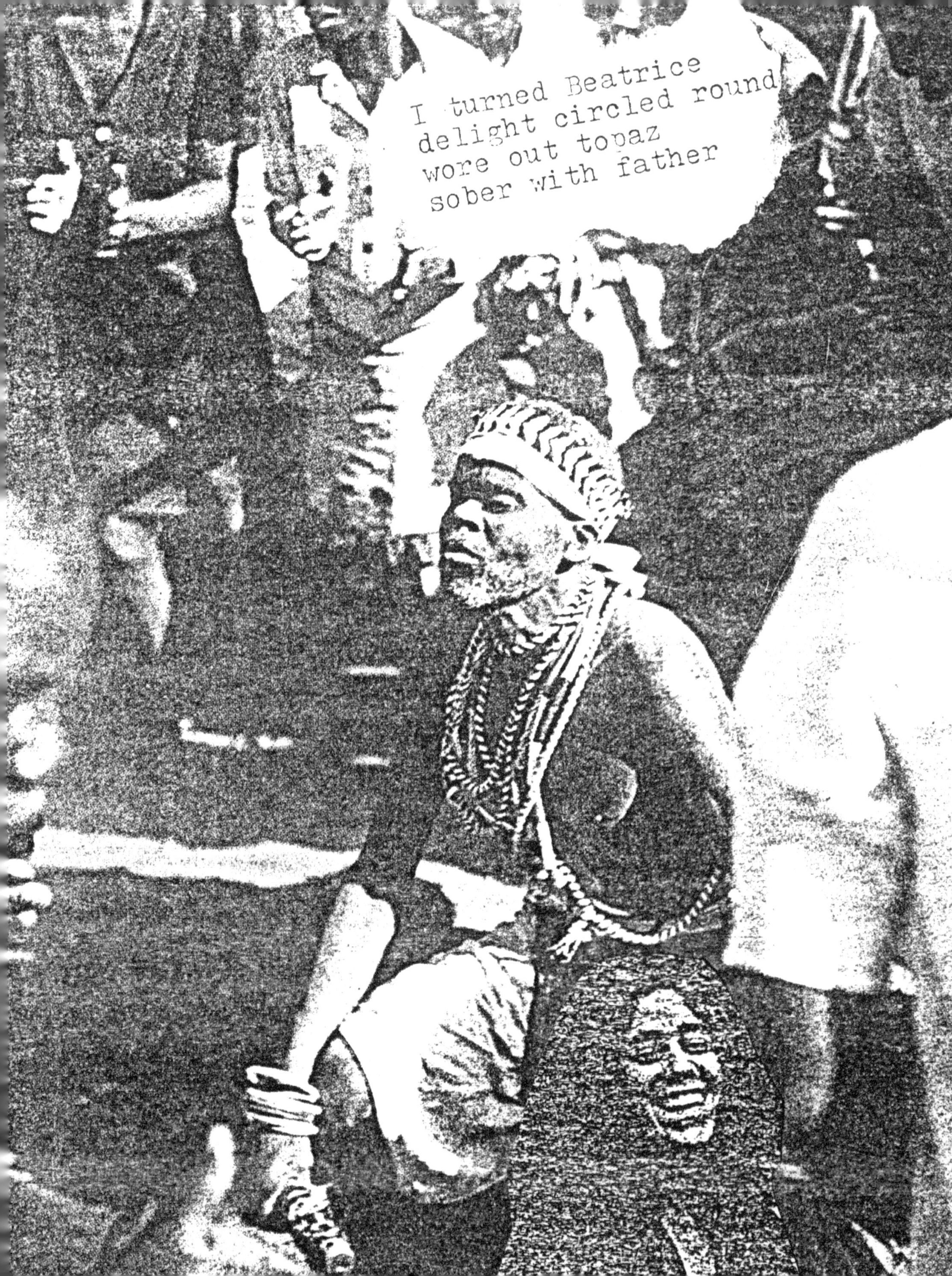
I turned Beatrice
delight circled round
wore out topaz
sober with father

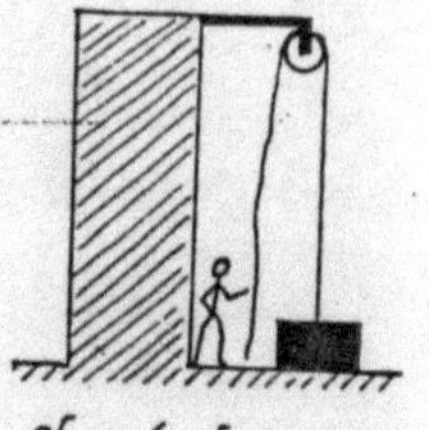
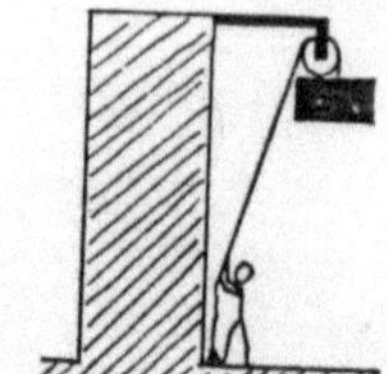
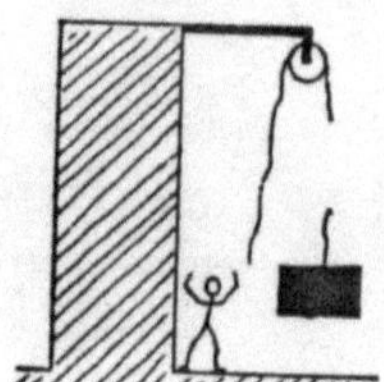
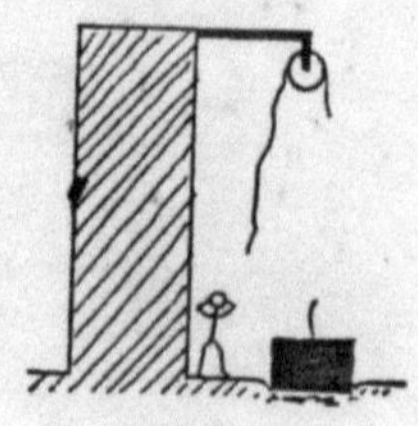

Chemical energy to gravitational P. E. to K. E. to heat

(via strain-energy in rope)

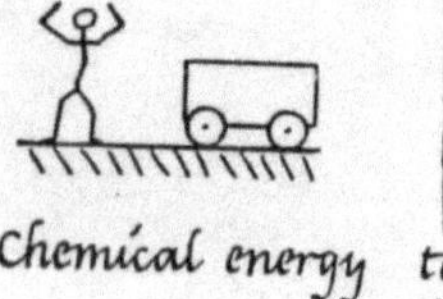
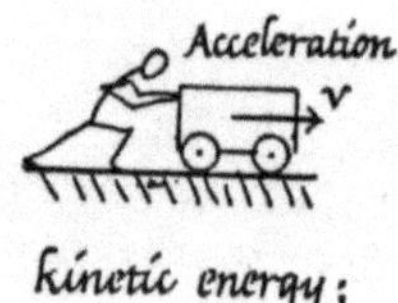

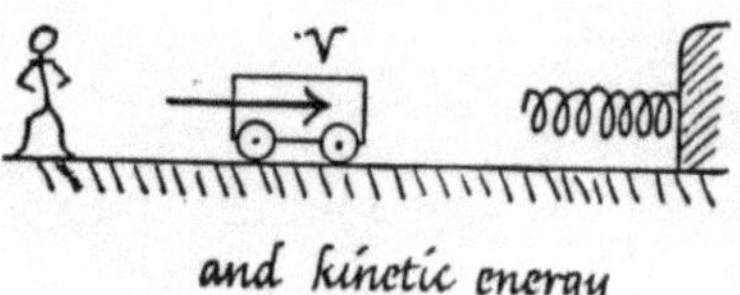

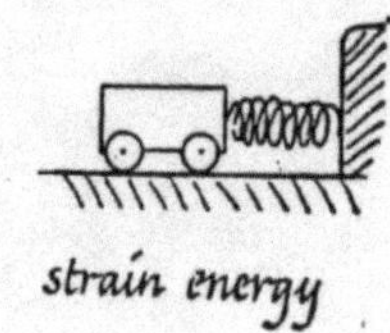

Chemical energy to kinetic energy; and kinetic energy to strain energy

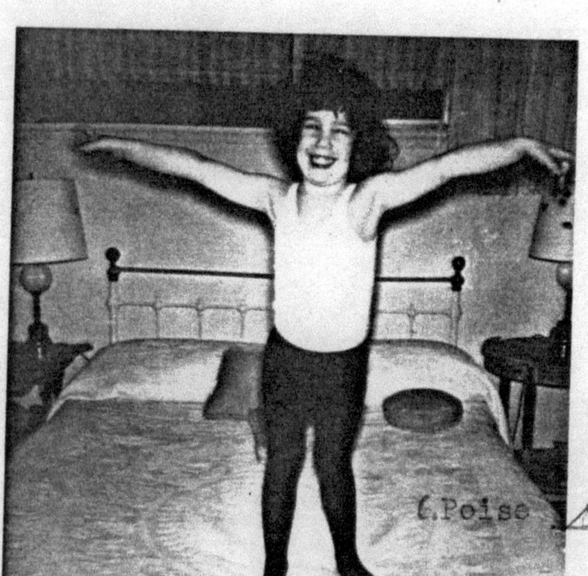
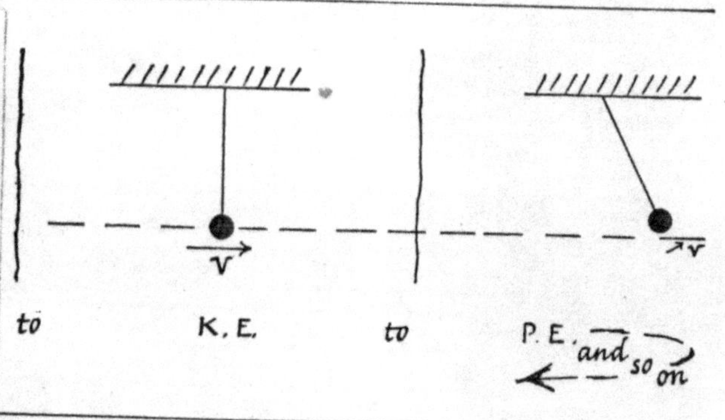

to K. E. to P. E. and so on

6.Poise

7. Voice Quality

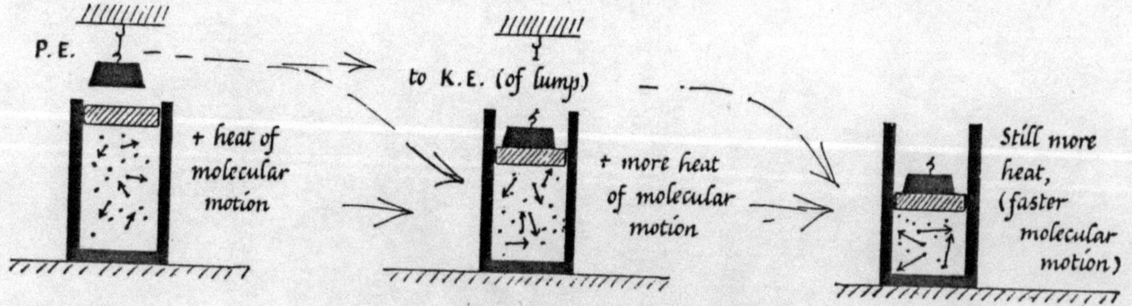

Fig. 26-32. Changes of Energy

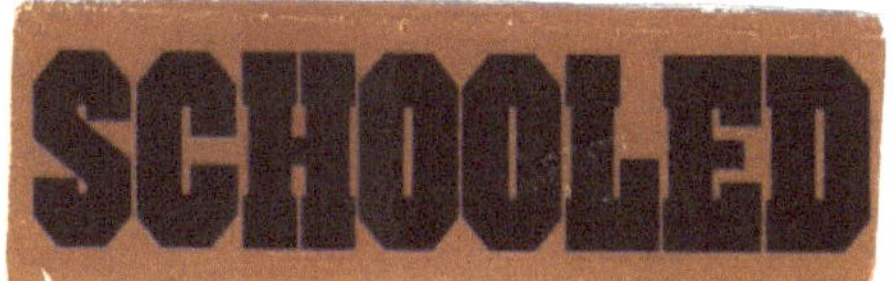

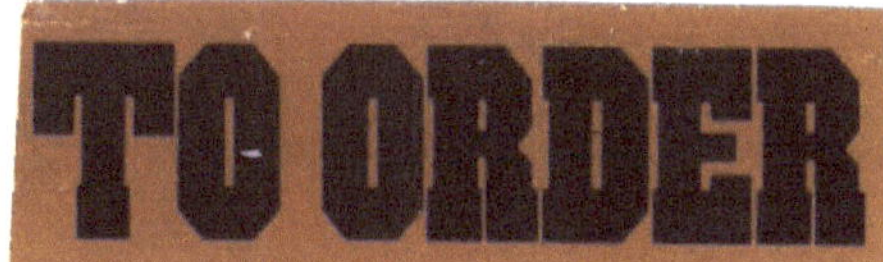

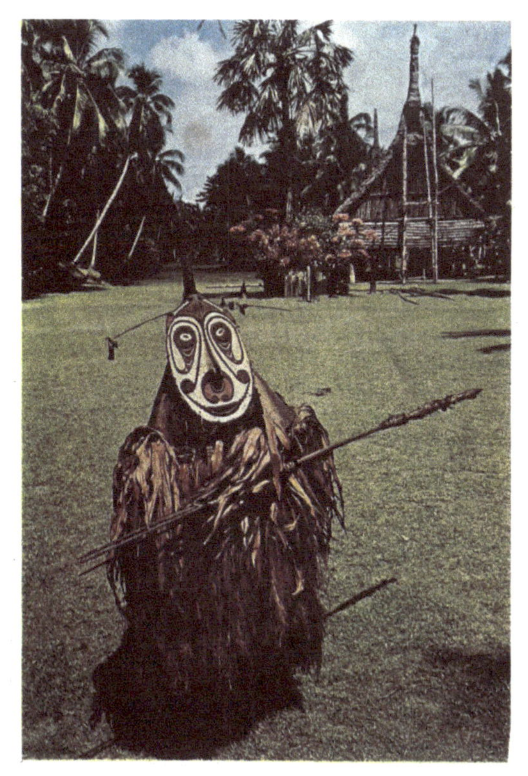

came the big thing. When it reached me, it went right over me. After it had gone, I had all different lines and shapes on me.

And from that day till now, I still have those lines and shapes.

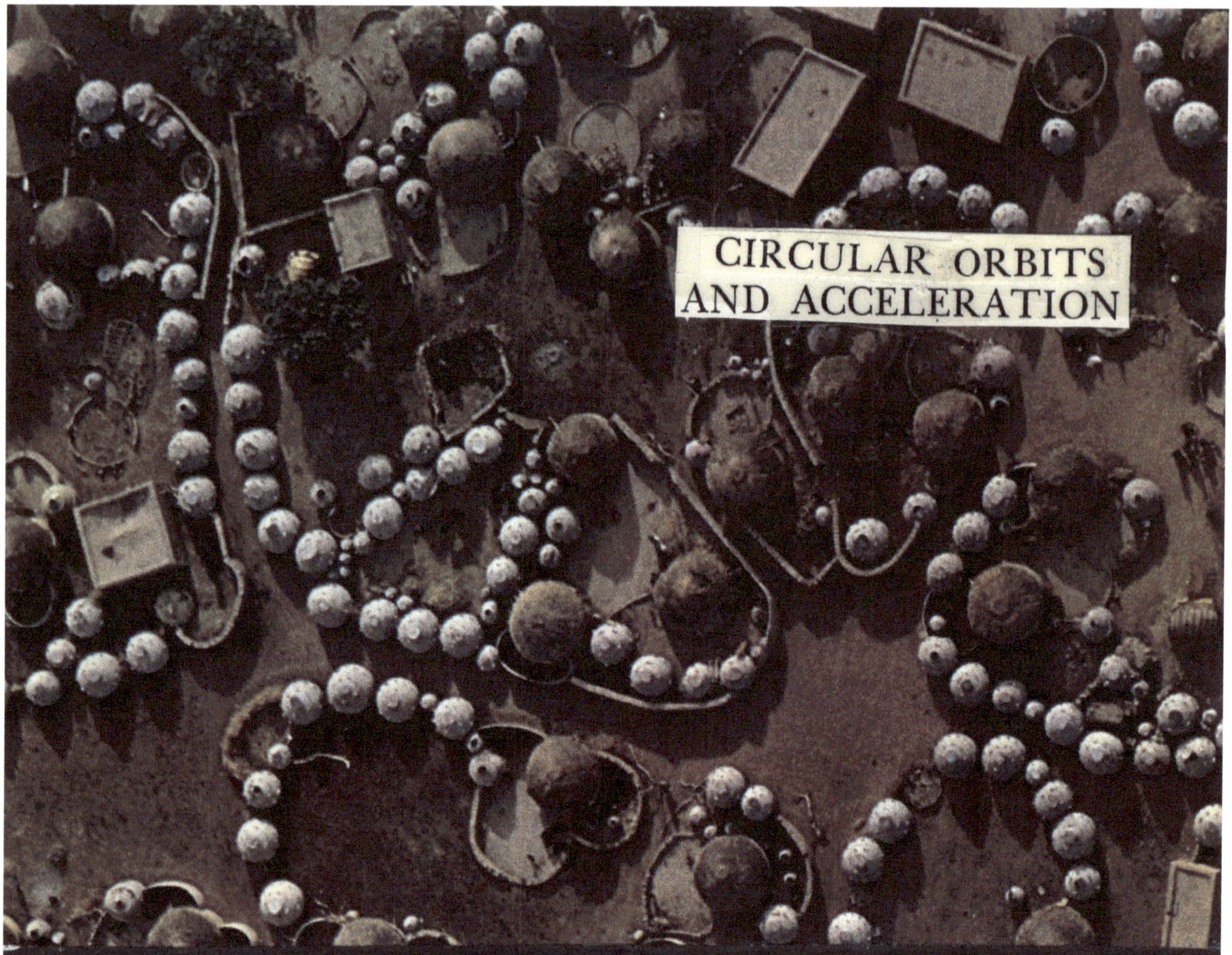

CIRCULAR ORBITS AND ACCELERATION

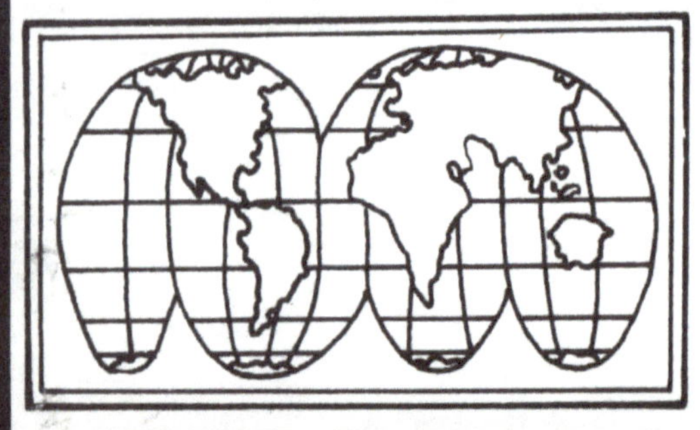

Where are you from?

I'm from ______________________

What are you?

I'm ______________________

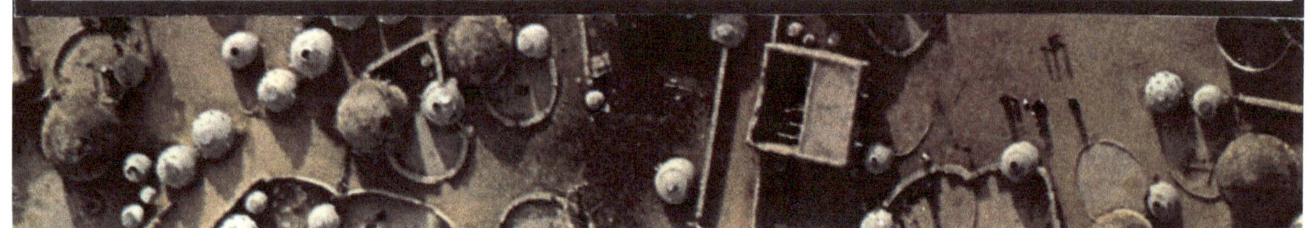

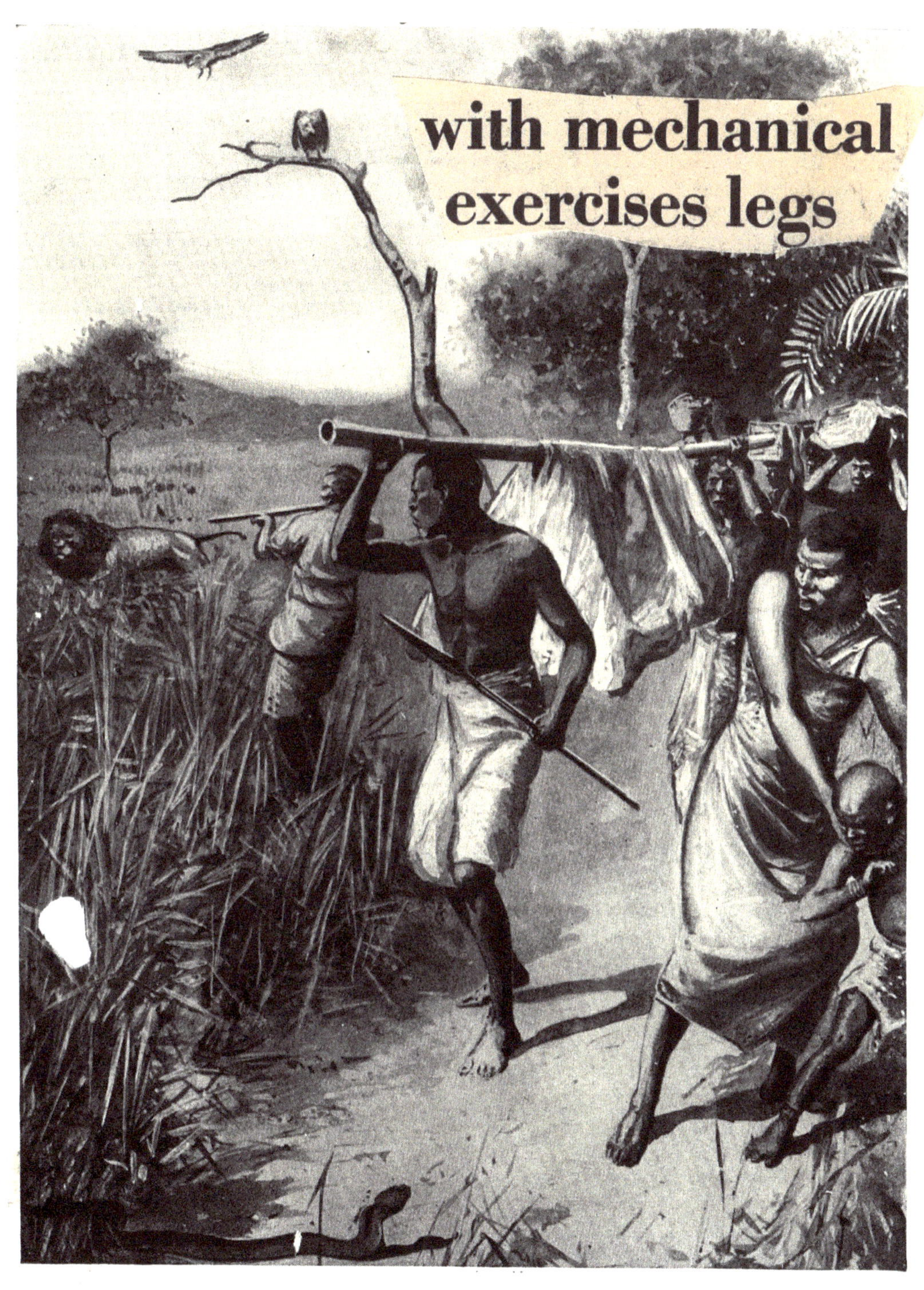
with mechanical
exercises legs

below for a rod (instead of ball) spinning in a uniform current of air. The pattern for a ball is somewhat similar.

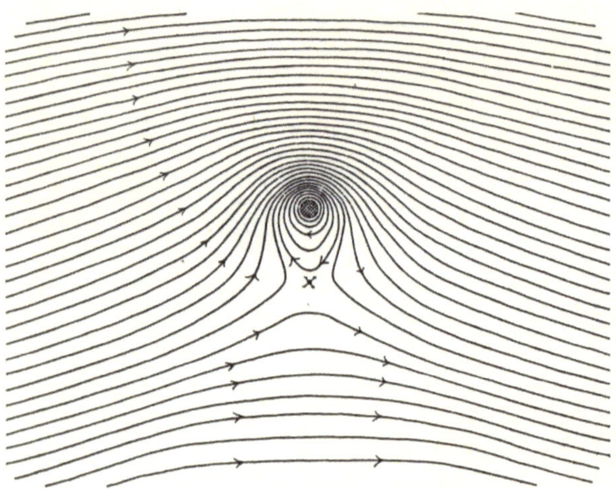

FIG. 9-21. STREAMLINES FOR A SPINNING CYLINDER IN UNIFORM WIND. These are sketched fairly accurately from the streamline pattern predicted geometrically from $\nabla^2 V = 0$, the basic mathematical rule governing streamline patterns of this kind and all other "inverse-square law" patterns.

PROBLEM 5

If you have studied physics before, you may have met this pattern in an entirely different part of physics. If so, where? Is the likeness purely coincidental? Can the likeness

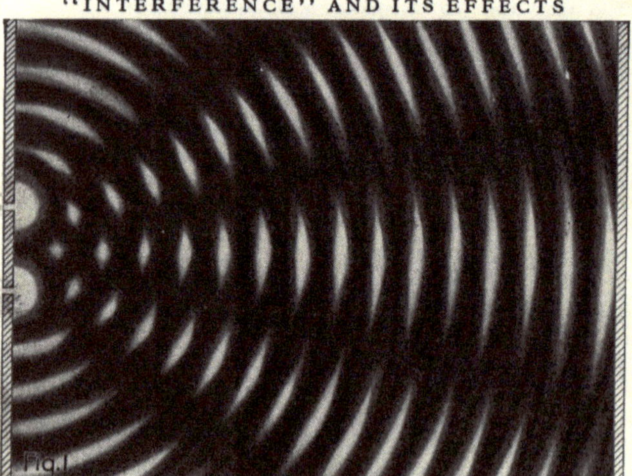

FIG. 9-22. PROBLEM 6. Streamlines for a source and an equal drain in an infinite lake of uniform depth.

In a huge shallow lake of still water, a spring at A delivers a steady inflow of water, and a drain at B carries away an equal outflow. Sketch the streamlines in the lake using the following help. The spring *by itself* would produce streamlines which are straight spokes radiating from A. Near A, where the streamlines are crowded close, the speed of this outflow along radii would be great. Farther out from A the speed would be smaller.* The drain *by itself* would produce a similar pattern of radial inflow to B.

Mark A and B a few inches apart on a full sheet of paper, sketch both sets of streamlines right across the paper and find the resultant pattern, by drawing and guessing. (What corresponds to hints (i, ii) above?)

Where have you met a similar pattern?

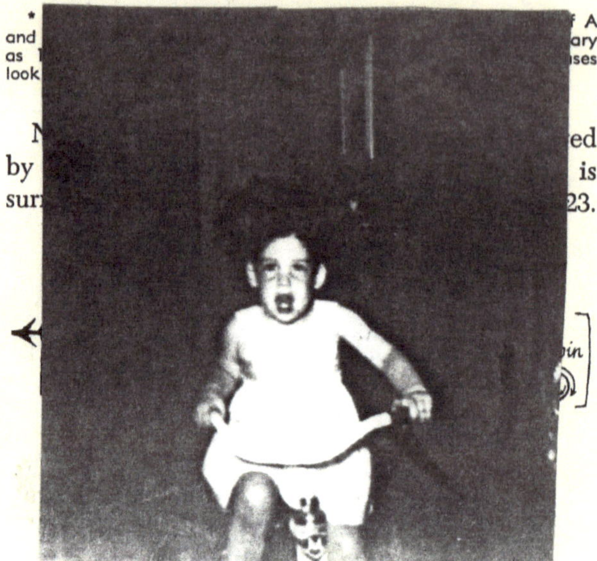

FIG. 9-23. STREAMLINES OF AIR FLOWING PAST A SPINNING BALL

Air is flowing past it faster above it than below it, so there is a region of lower pressure above it and high pressure below. Air pressure therefore pushes the ball upward, distorting its path. Similarly a ball with a spin around a vertical axis is pushed to one side and will swerve. There have been many arguments about this matter, but the "curving" of a spinning baseball has been measured. However, prejudice from a pitcher's reputation may make player or spectator see more curves than are there. With a lighter ball spinning fast—e.g. a cut tennis ball—real curves are easily seen.

★ PROBLEM 7. THROWING CURVES

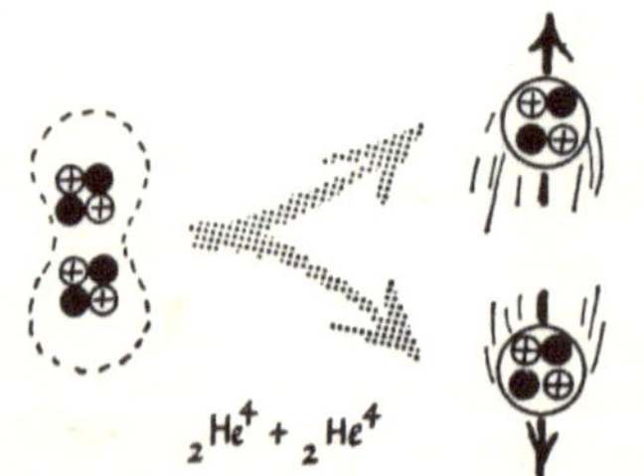

(vii) A cork ball is thrown across the room from a rough cardboard tube. The thrower holds the tube behind his shoulder, and slings the ball out by

Plants

In fall, cork grows around the stem of a leaf. It squeezes the stem so the leaf turns color. When the cork [illegible] the stem, the cork [illegible] er. It grows so heav[illegible] af falls to the g[illegible] e leaves

TEPEE

A tepee is made o

they were
all anothers
cleanliness
stink of shit

An igloo is made
f ice and snow. Eski
mos lived in an Igloo

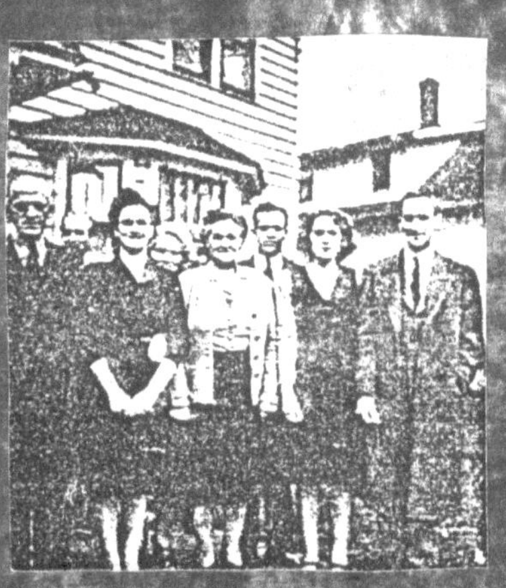

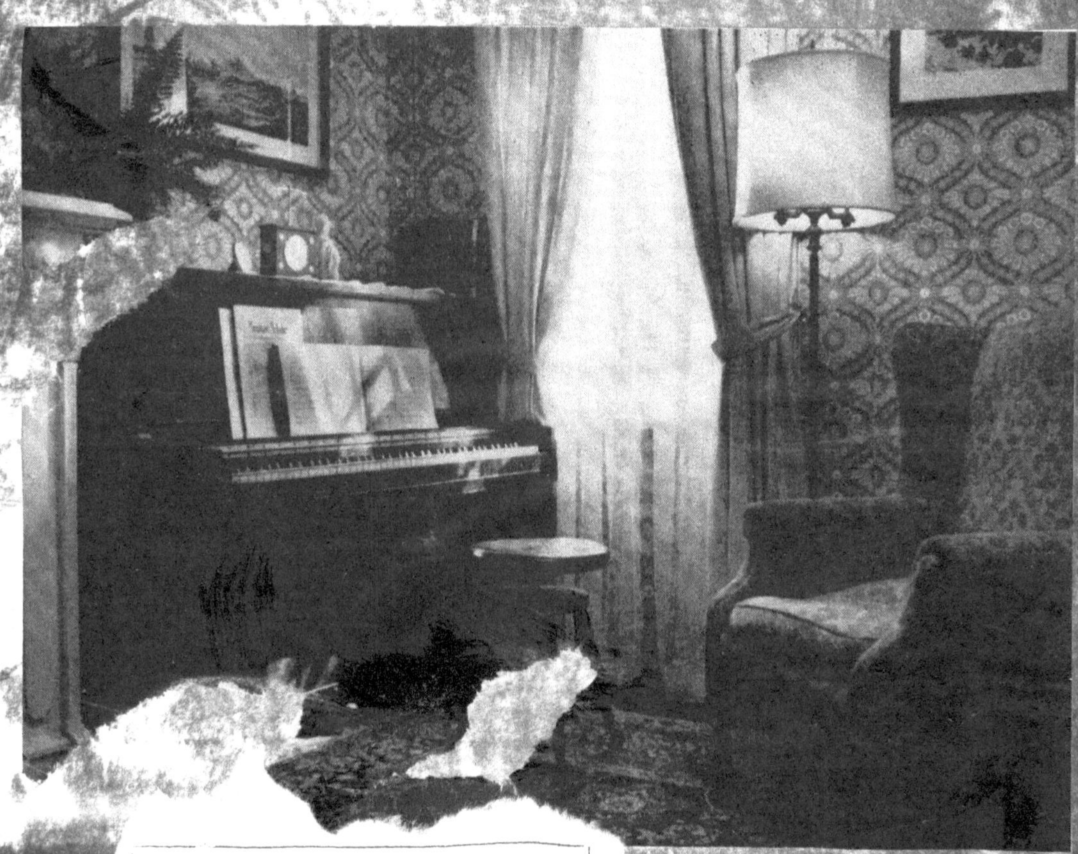

IRREVERSIBLE EXPANSION

TO EACH NEW GENERATION

the reason for my inability to verbalyze my feelings to you and your Mother concerning the variety of events surrounding my last visit to Roslyn

Decorating: all in the mind

on the cutting board. The incredible contradictions reflected in the wealth of that area. What I wanted so hard to ask your Mother was how you Nasaw's could be such decent people amidst all the others. People like you just don't grow on trees. When I left Roslyn I heaved a sigh of relief and said, "I'll never go back there again". I rationalyzed my inability to sit down and talk things out though my rationalyzations were transparent as Saran wrap. It was so much easier for me to blame others, but deep down I knew who the transgressor was. I felt so defeated that I wanted to lay down and croak. And I just about did that when I became deathly ill in Cleveland. Now I think it was psychosomatic.

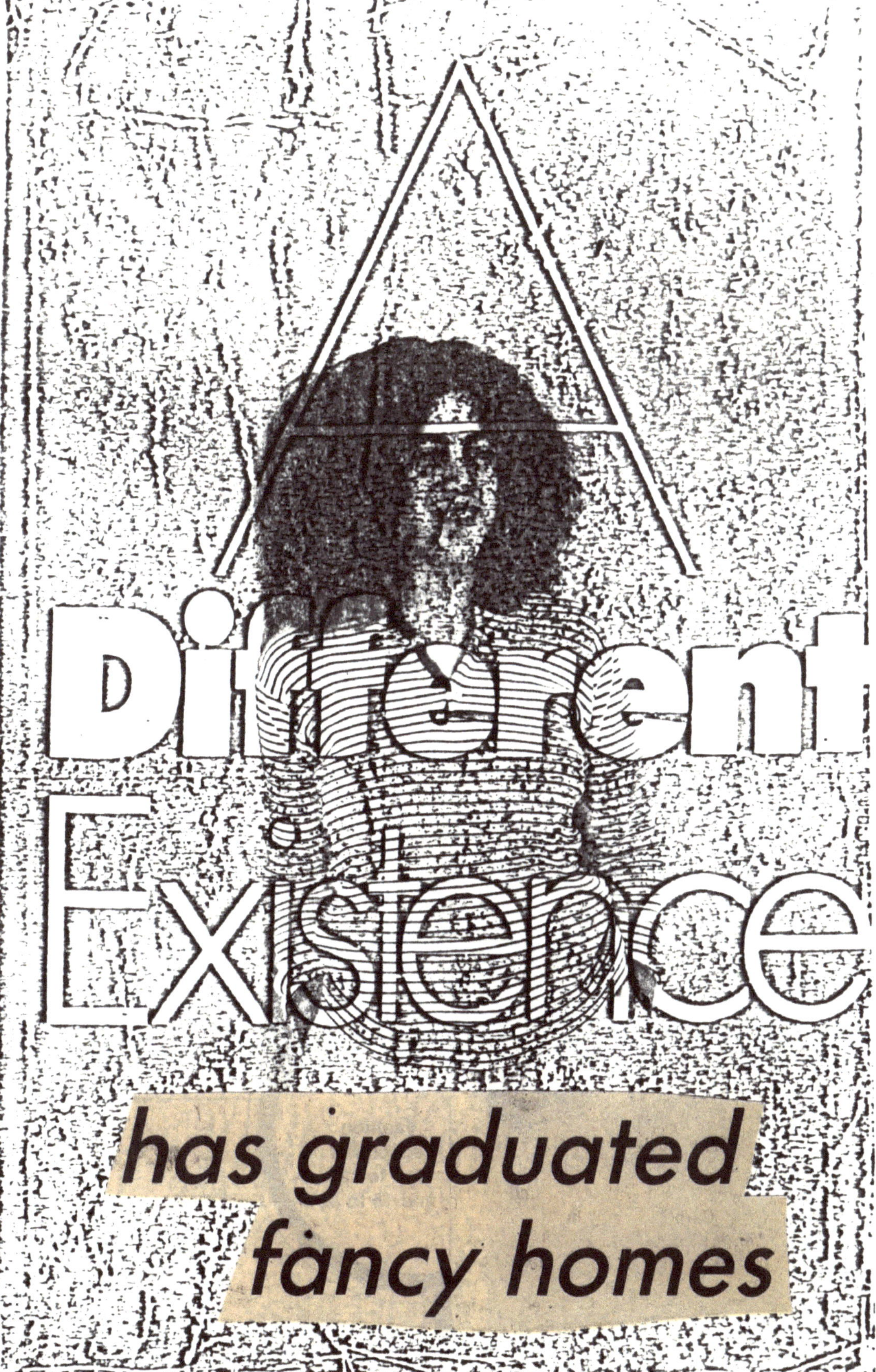
Different
Existence
has graduated
fancy homes

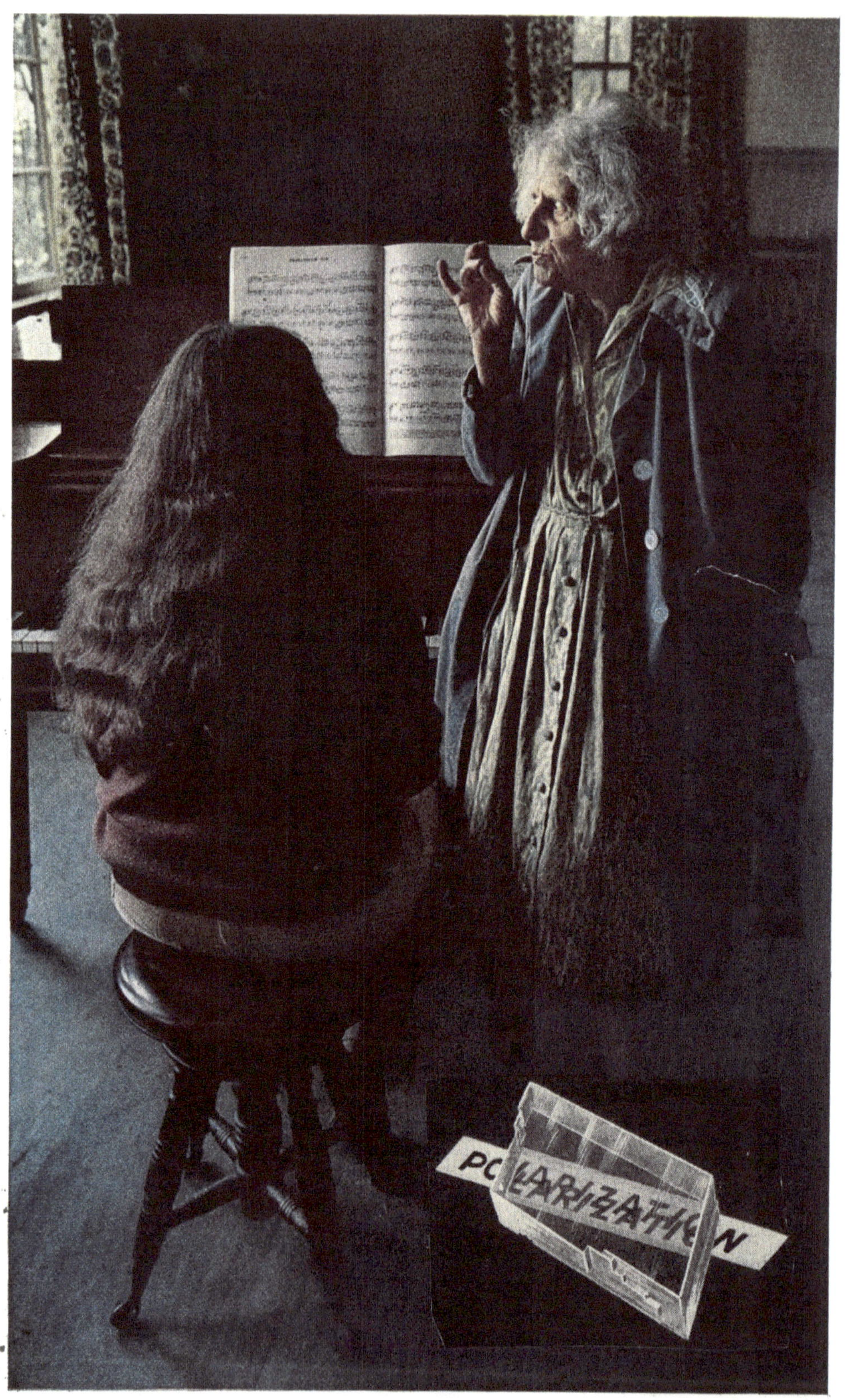

reverse roles

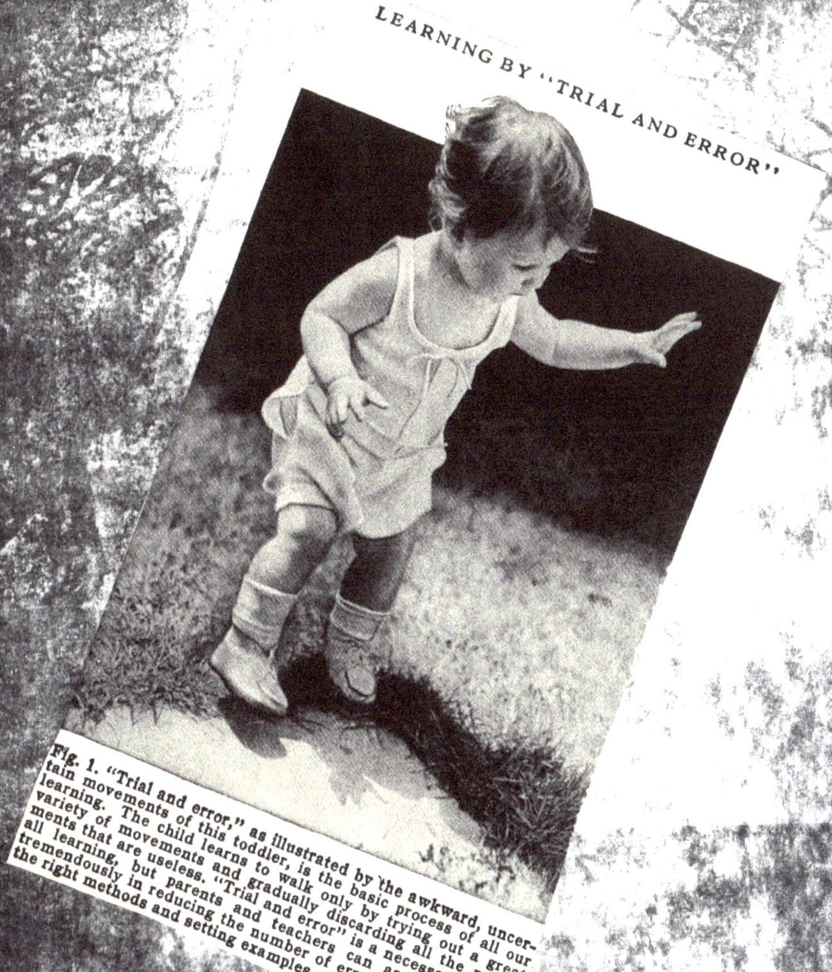

Change Ripples New

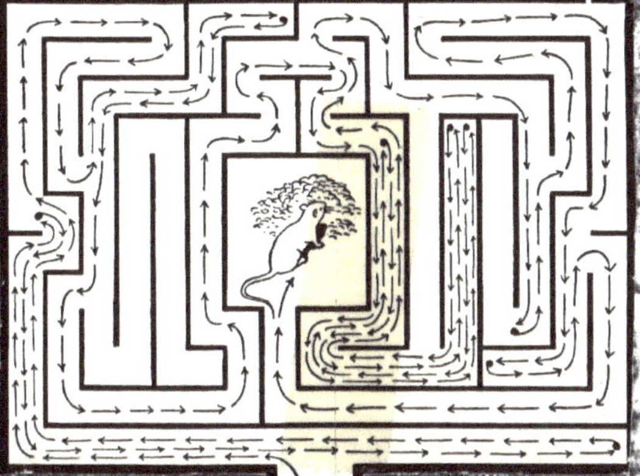

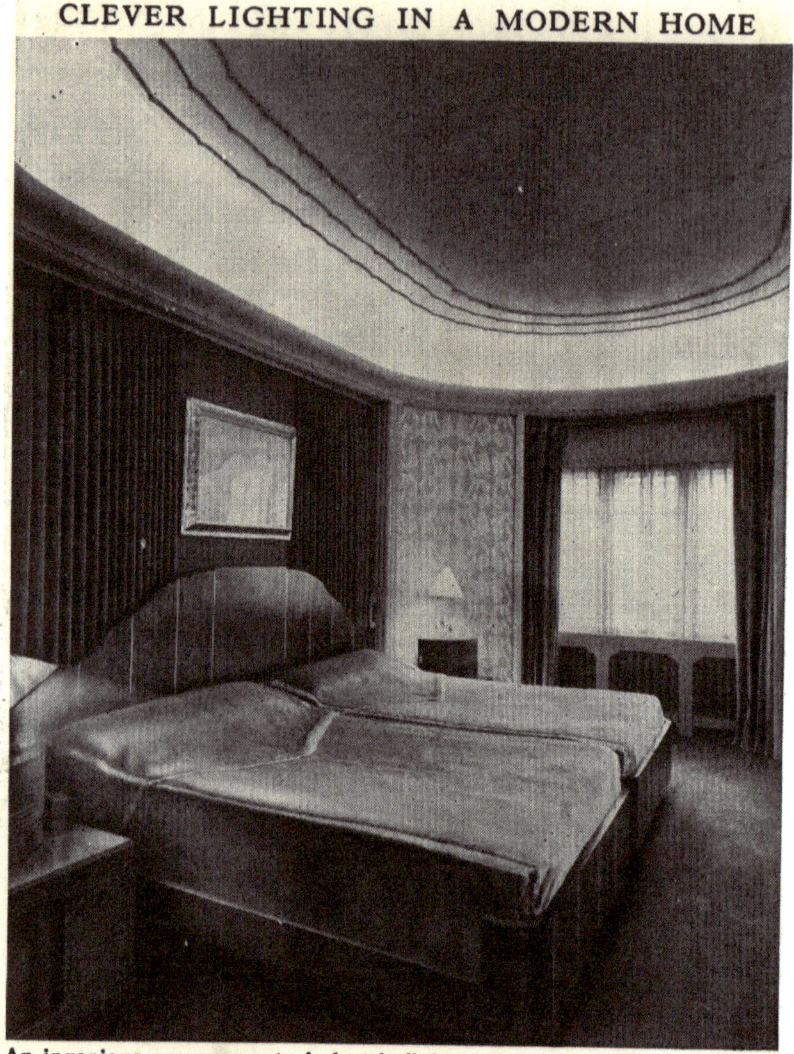

CLEVER LIGHTING IN A MODERN HOME

An ingenious arrangement of electric lights concealed behind a molding gives a soft light throughout this ultramodern room. Two shaded lamps provide centers of interest and avoid the banality which comes from a flood of shadow-banishing light reaching every corner.

hearing shall keep us
stripped of flesh
come less quickly
more piercing

obscure after sparks
in itself directed
pleasure decked out

kilos-

i've hesitated to write you only because i have too much to say. perhaps it'd be better to say nothing at all. or best, wait for a dialogue... i hope you can feel across the ocean that of course i think of you often — & how could i possibly forget your shit? i took a sip of ~~[illegible]~~ melon-sweet whine ~~wine~~ the other day, reading the Symposium. i feel about you as Alcibiades feels about Soc. (i, however, ain't gonna sell out.). and what better thing to tell the stinging ladder-that's-left-behind but: i am good, really good. i live on, & up.

Rural wedding conforms to the rhythm of the farm

... i can only add the com-
... ~~[illegible]~~ short. ~~[illegible]~~ to
... to feel too much
like a holiday inn. needless to say, i won't extend the reservation.
i'm anxious to shed my "social identity," to tingle once again w/ the fear of flying. i need to recall the sense that there's just me & the world, nothing else. i wish i could suck this place bone dry
before i leave, though. ... 's
free width," & enjoyed it. ... is.
we've become quite close; ... afternoon
when i jam w/ him, & he ... relaxing
times. he asks of you ... unwise-
ly. in turn, i suggest to you ... "...lists".
i've devoted this term to ... read me
to this book. havelock ... but he
did it thoroughly. it's a different kind of thing than cushman but i think very important.

i really like the Lysis, but trying to declare a favorite dialogue is like trying to do only one bong hit at a sitting. shit what's it like being straight? i can't imagine it, is it like being high, at first? i'm sure it'd do me some good some day. (not today she says as she reaches for the crumpled baggie.) when i'm not busy rolling seeds down a cardboard mountain ~~or~~ or looking "under leaves" for matches (no kidding — i know this guy ben w/ whom i was once tripping at →

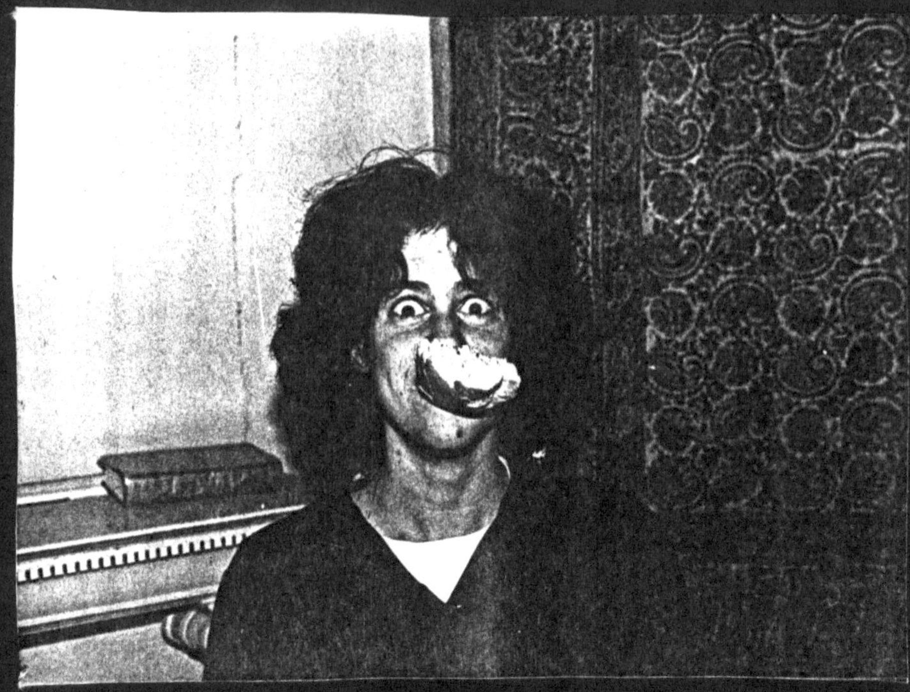

School —
Within —
A —
School

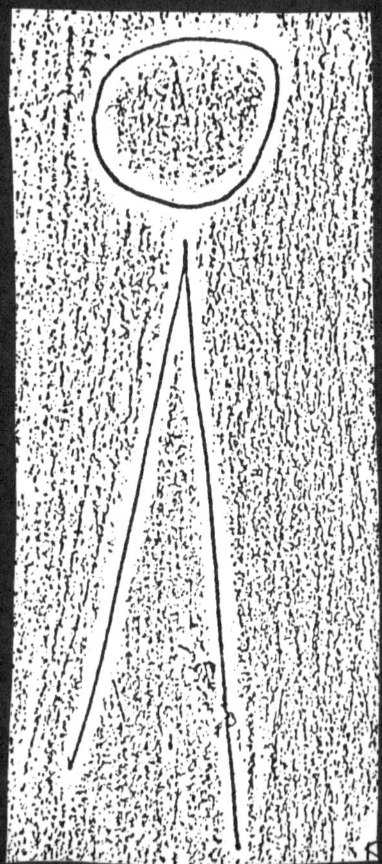

Philosophy in the Middle

Common Activity Scale

Prescriptiveness	Controls	Physical Movement
Low	Low	High
High	High	Low
Low	Low	Low
Low	Low	Medium
Low	Medium	Low
High	High	Low
Medium	High	Low
Medium	Medium	Low
High	High	Medium–High
Medium	Medium	High
Medium	High	High
Low–Medium	Medium	Medium
Low	Low	High
Medium	Medium	High
Low	Low	High
Medium	Medium	Medium–High
High	High	Medium
High	High	Medium
Low	Medium	Medium
High	High	Low
High	High	Low
High	High	Low

Philosophy is as ... s to a person as it
is somehting that he ... vent in which the tran-
sformer is himself t ... ot, strictly speaking,
be separated from th ... ay--not even Socrates
himself, who of cour ... ere tis Socrates, let
us watch him philoso ... n him his philosophy."
One must say instead ... Philosophy. Let us
become of this ring ... ere let the song sing
itself."

Socrates does not ... y, take it if you
will."; but rather,"Here I am where are you?" Or, as Zarathustra
said, "Here is my way where is yours?" This query, which is really
a demand, is th ... adfly. What is
painful is that ... aterial which has
been associated ... back off to sleep
by means of a s ... particular "way"
that is being c ... fended, urged and
demanded is no ... l response to
the human need ... the solution to
a problem, but ... , implications,
and most of all ... , "I disagree,"
he can only say ... this seriously."
The greatest ph ... Plato and Nietzsche
consist in the ... cross every sleepers
path to the re

(And what is truly sublime about Nietsche is that he did not take
the problems of philosophy

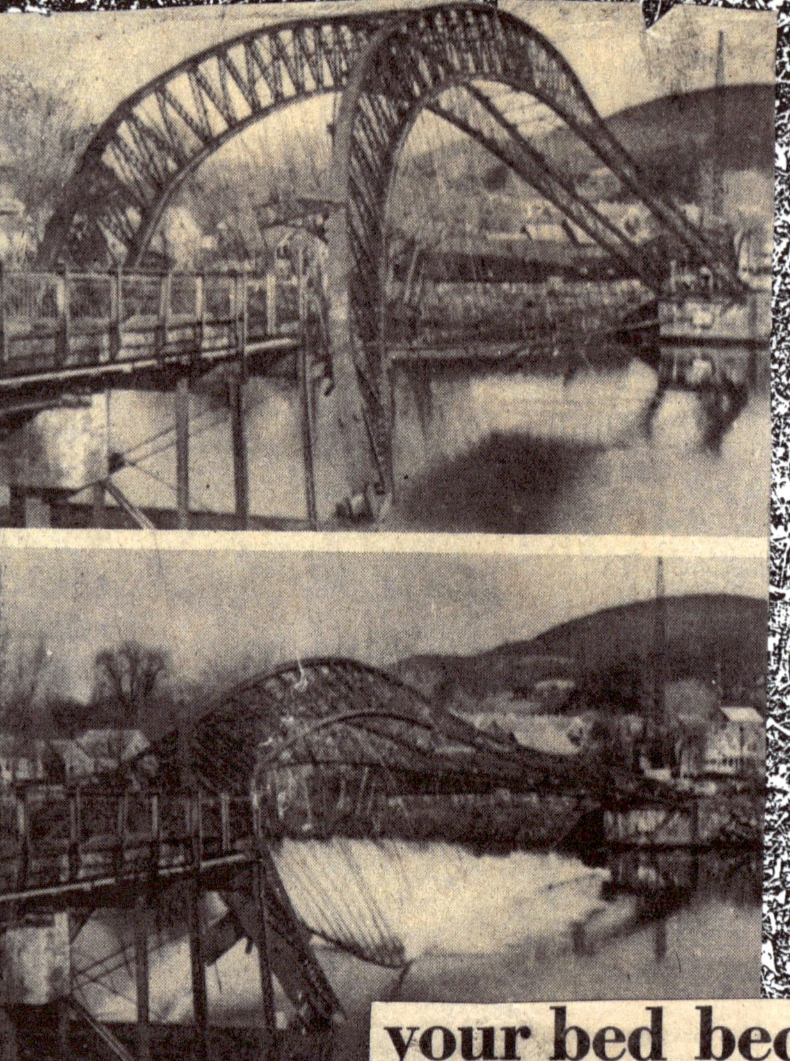

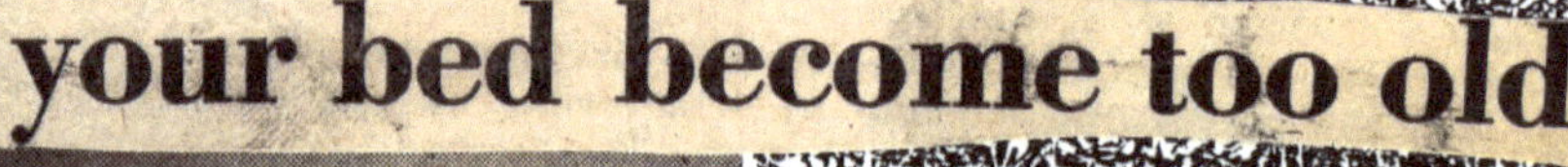
your bed become too old

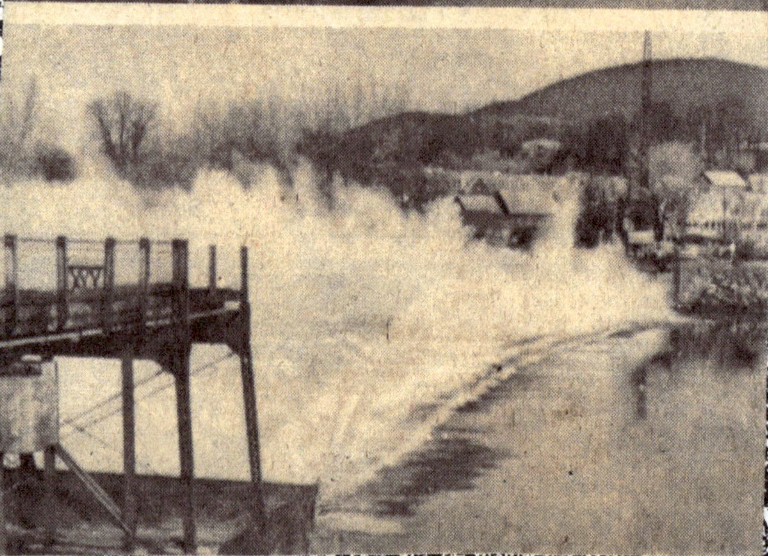

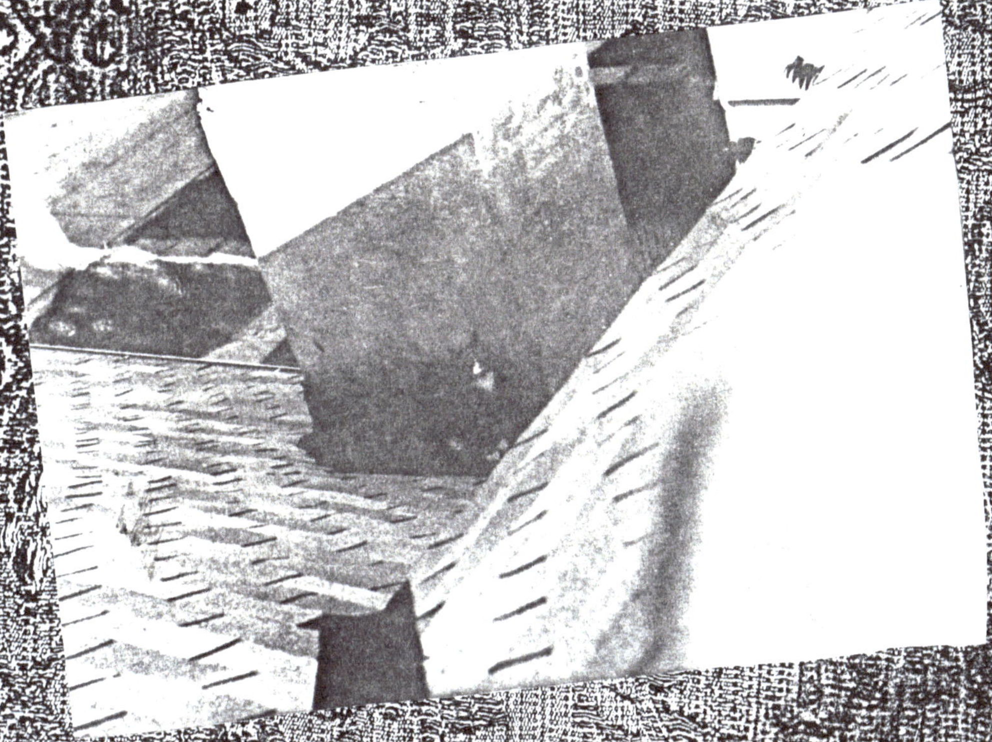

sustained family

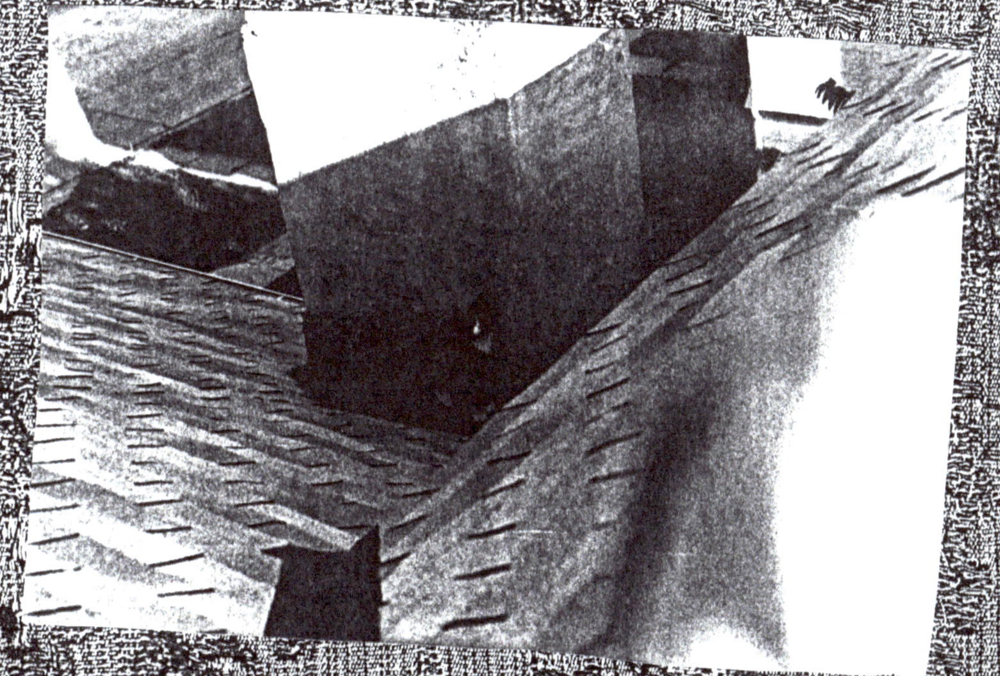

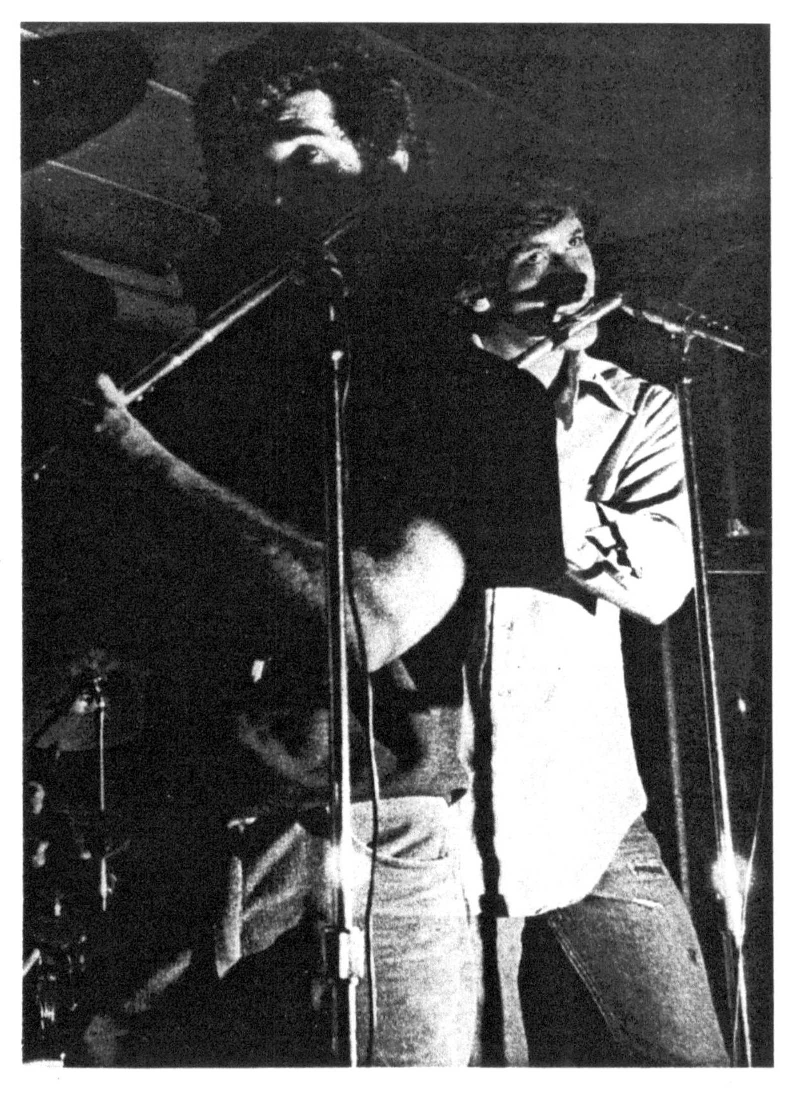

pan and melted it.

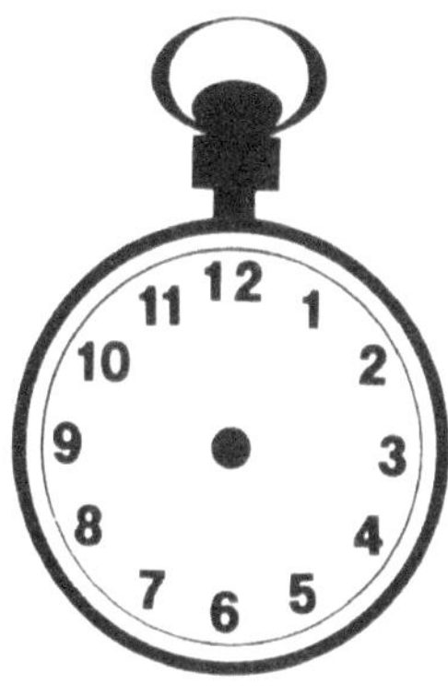

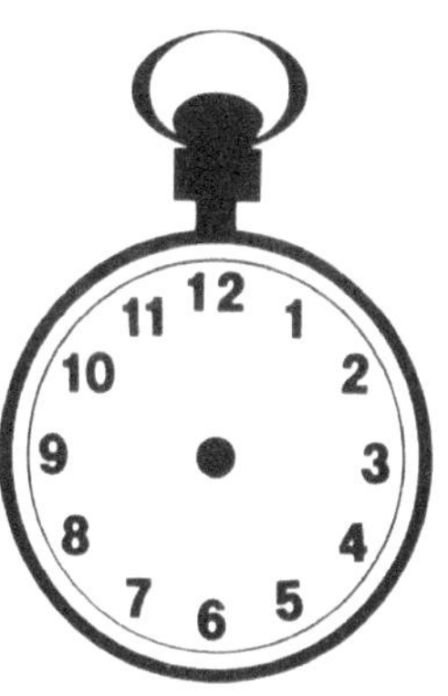

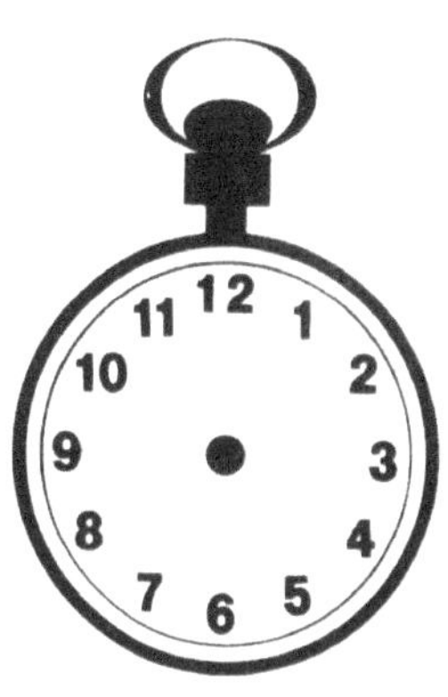

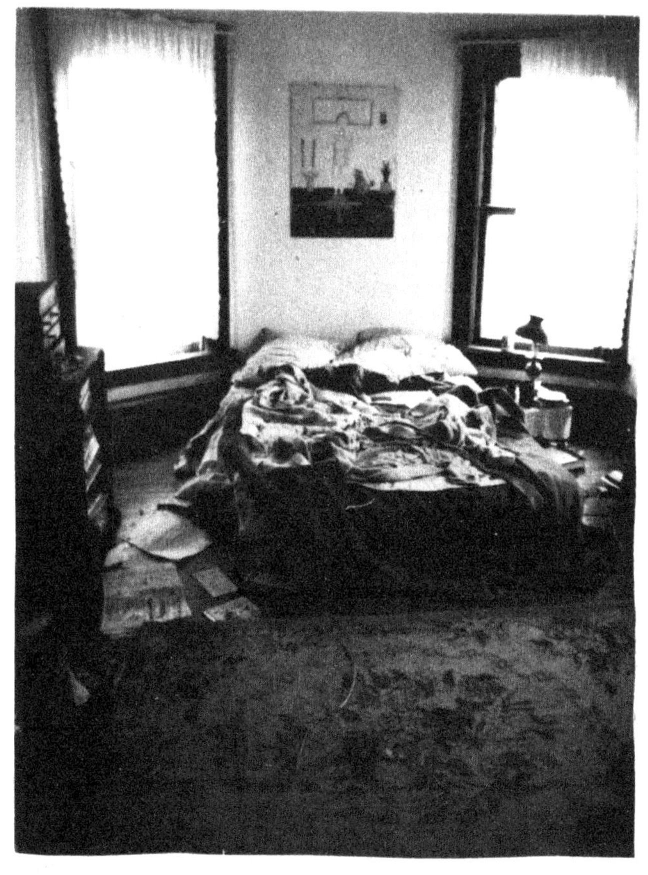

the face

near miss

dreamy conditiondx

on my back

it never once

resent you

what-have-you

have chaged

~~he cheeks me~~

out on the controls

dark winter afternoon

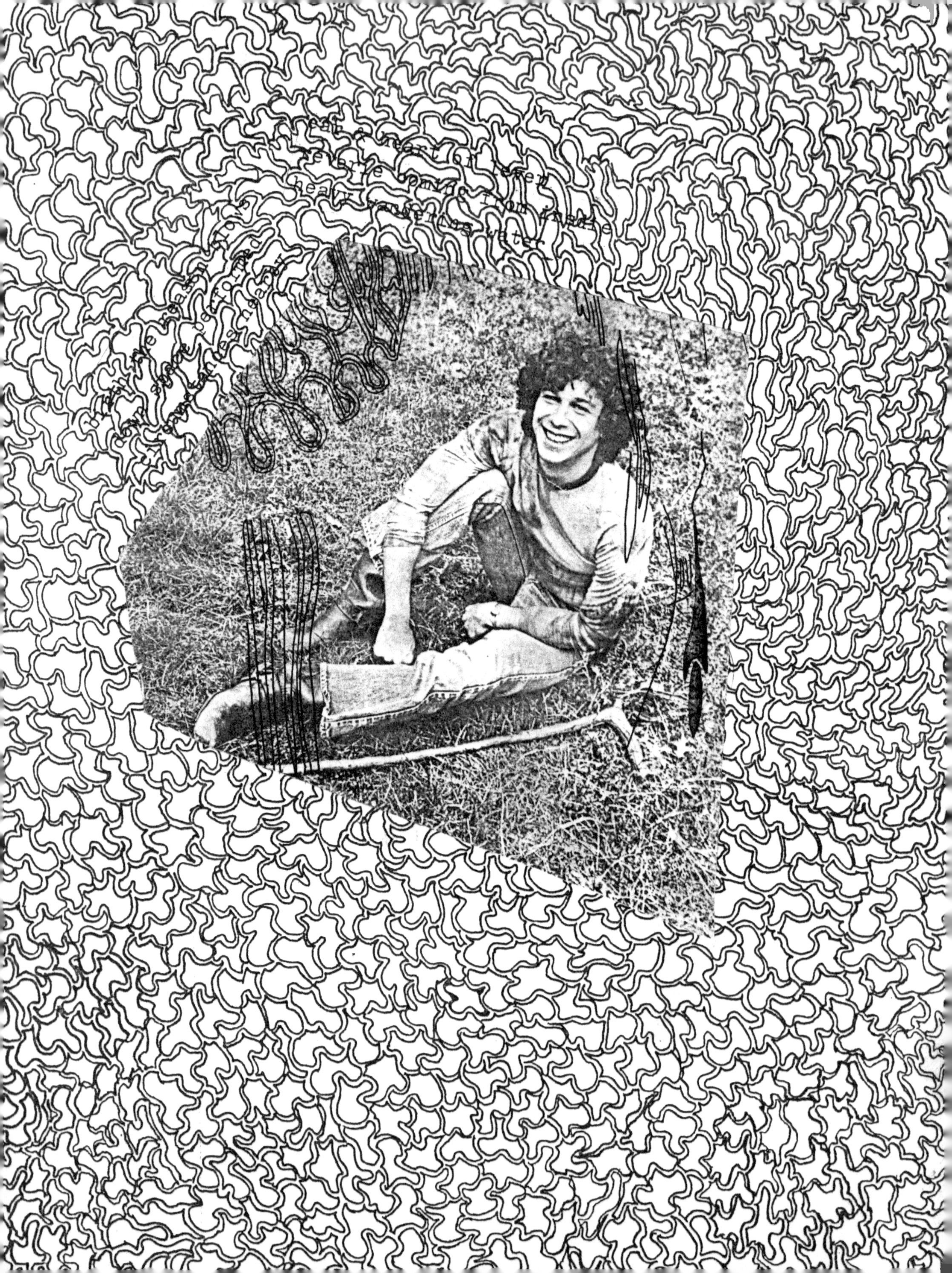
eat a heart of fever
reverie coming from inside
heavy wandering water

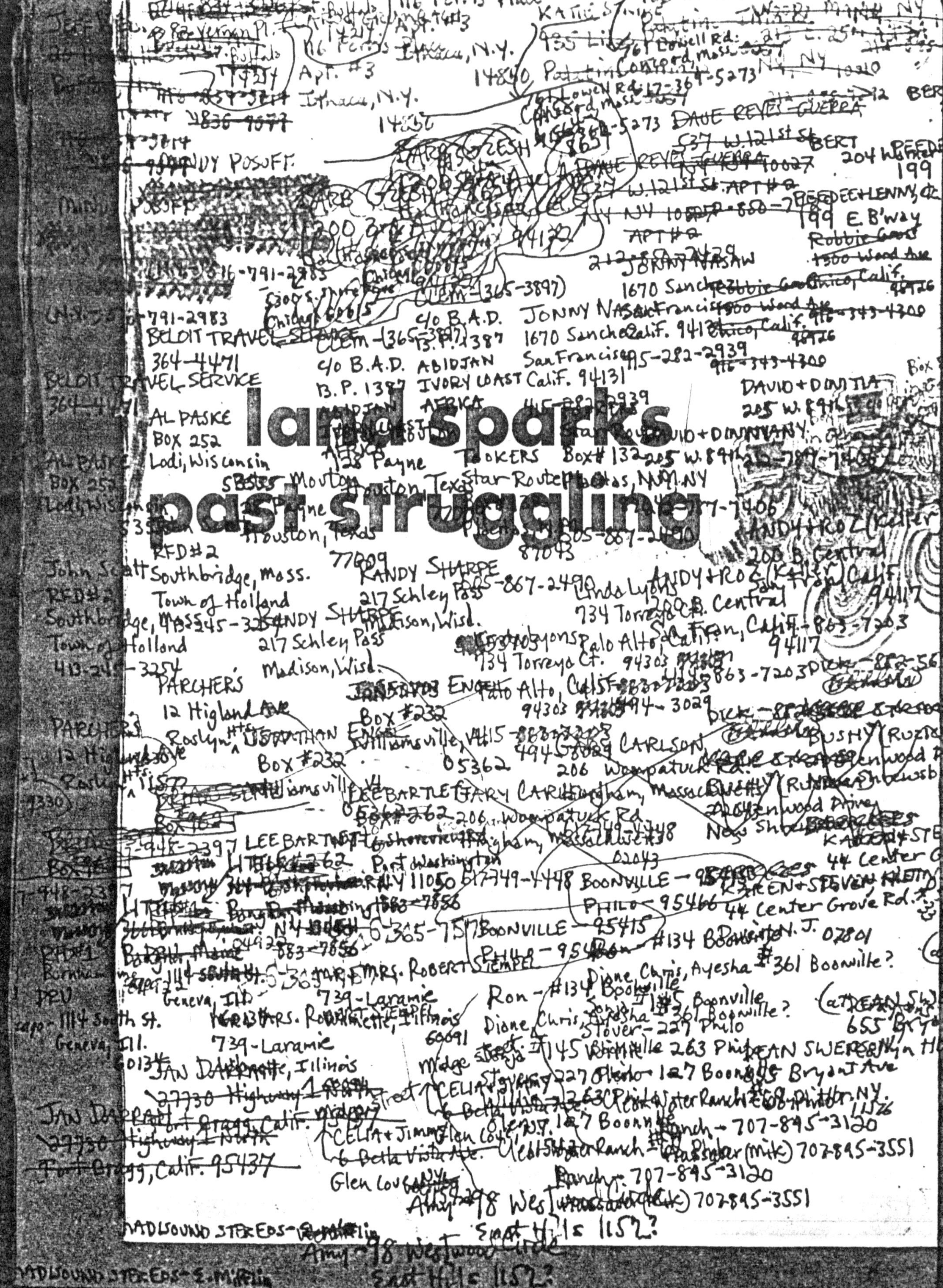
land sparks
past struggling

Dear Diz, 9/30/79

Glad to get yr. letter. Was going to call you at first but yr. phone never got answered. I think it's terrific that you are going to dedicate yr. not inconsiderable energies to the great god music. I really don't think ~~Hey~~ there's anything better anybody can do with their life than be an artist & it doesn't really matter which discipline you follow, though I suppose it's easiest when it's the one you have the most talent for. Which in yr. case is certainly music & I wish you luck. Meher Baba said (or wrote, or pointed to on his letter-board, as he didn't talk after, oh I don't know, around nineteen-thirty), "Music is the seventh shadow of the Word." And that's pretty high -- he never ever mentioned novels.

But I have to tell you, I never realized I'd started anything so big when I used to go into yr. [illegible] & I was thirteen & [illegible] dy in the key of C. And you know I think my favorite instrument is the saxophone -- particularly a nice simple hard-blowing King Curtis or Clarence

impression

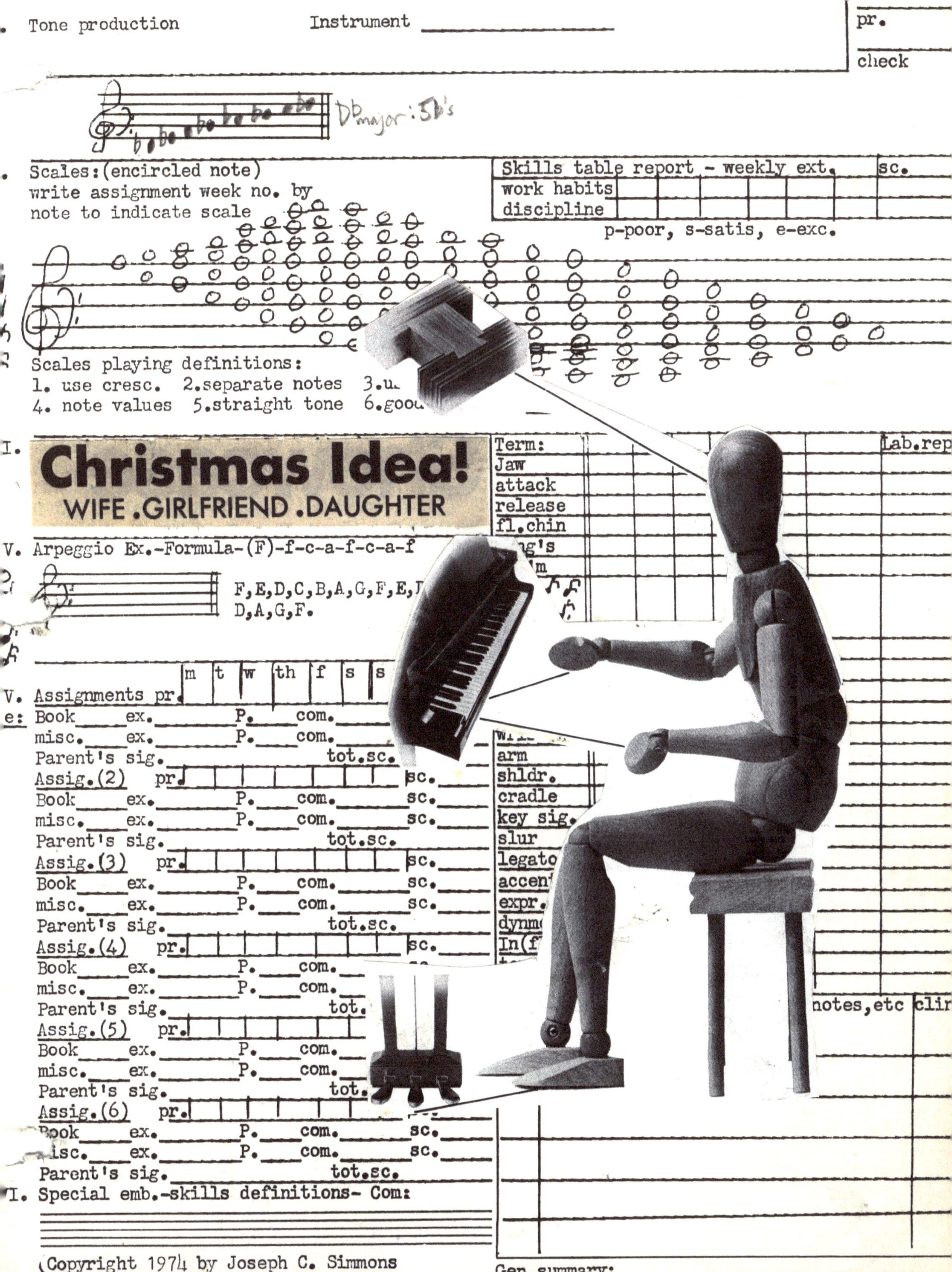

Tone production
Instrument
pr.
check
Db major: 5b's
Scales: (encircled note)
write assignment week no. by
note to indicate scale
Skills table report - weekly ext.
sc.
work habits
discipline
p-poor, s-satis, e-exc.
Scales playing definitions:
1. use cresc.
2. separate notes
4. note values
5. straight tone
Christmas Idea!
WIFE .GIRLFRIEND .DAUGHTER
Term:
Jaw
attack
release
fl. chin
Lab. rep
V. Arpeggio Ex.-Formula-(F)-f-c-a-f-c-a-f
D,A,G,F.
m t w th f s s
V. Assignments pr.
Book ex. P. com.
misc. ex. P. com.
Parent's sig. tot. sc.
Assig. (2) pr. sc.
Assig. (3) pr. sc.
Assig. (4) pr. sc.
Assig. (5) pr.
Assig. (6) pr.
arm
shldr.
cradle
key sig.
slur
notes, etc
I. Special emb.-skills definitions- Com:
Copyright 1974 by Joseph C. Simmons
Gen. summary:

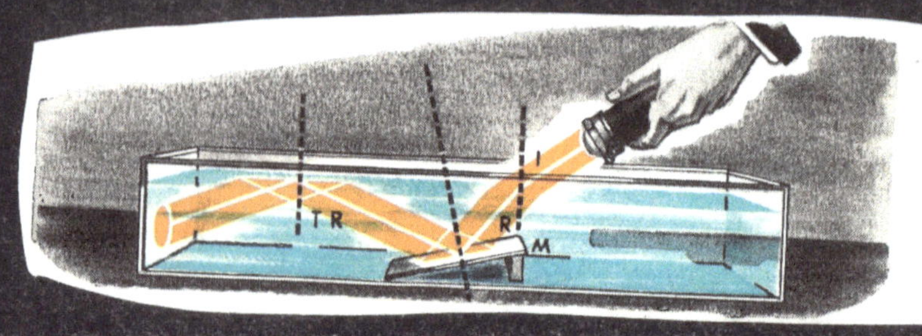

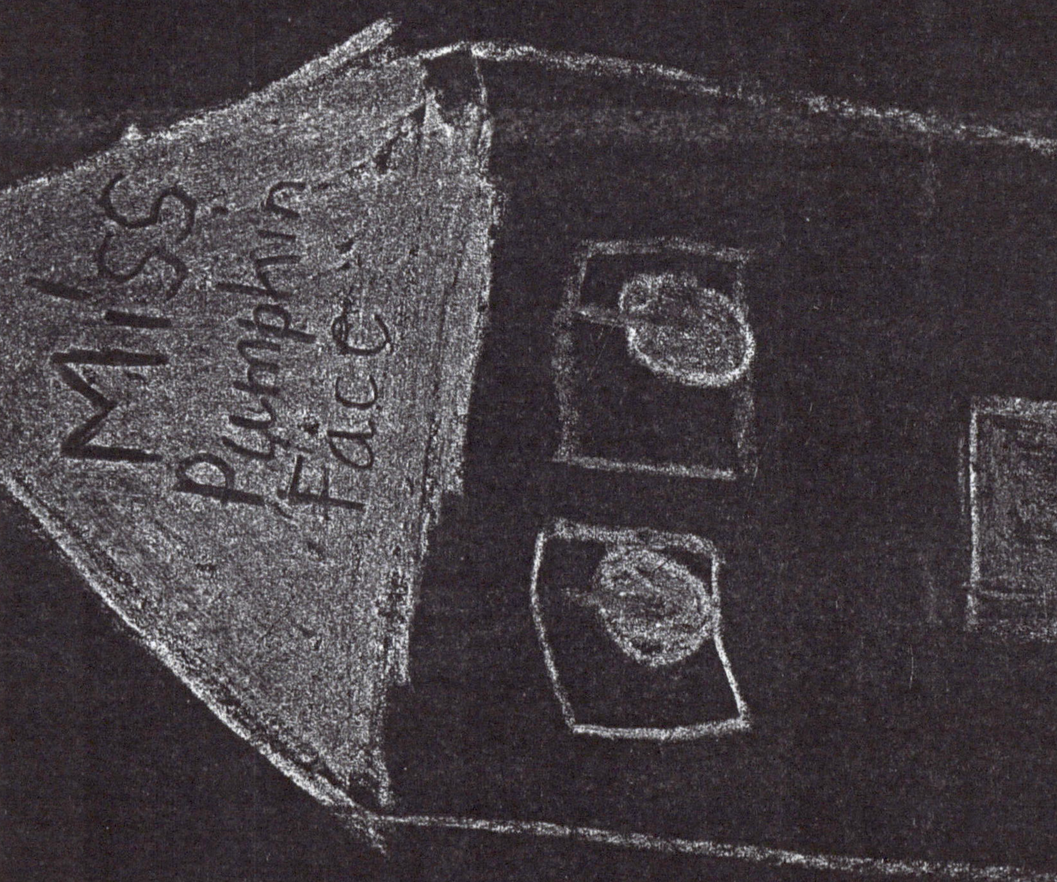

lay big brick in

But what about all the seeds. buried under snow. Unless you are frozen solid now, if not the junk yard), ordinary cool bulb is the sun, but seedlings concentrate on the spirit. Still meet, exchange information, and share musical ideas with friend, or relative, or labor. Soak them in water overnight.

If we are in need of healing, birth occurs. Over and over out; it means coming to know soil, and the greater the health means always learning.

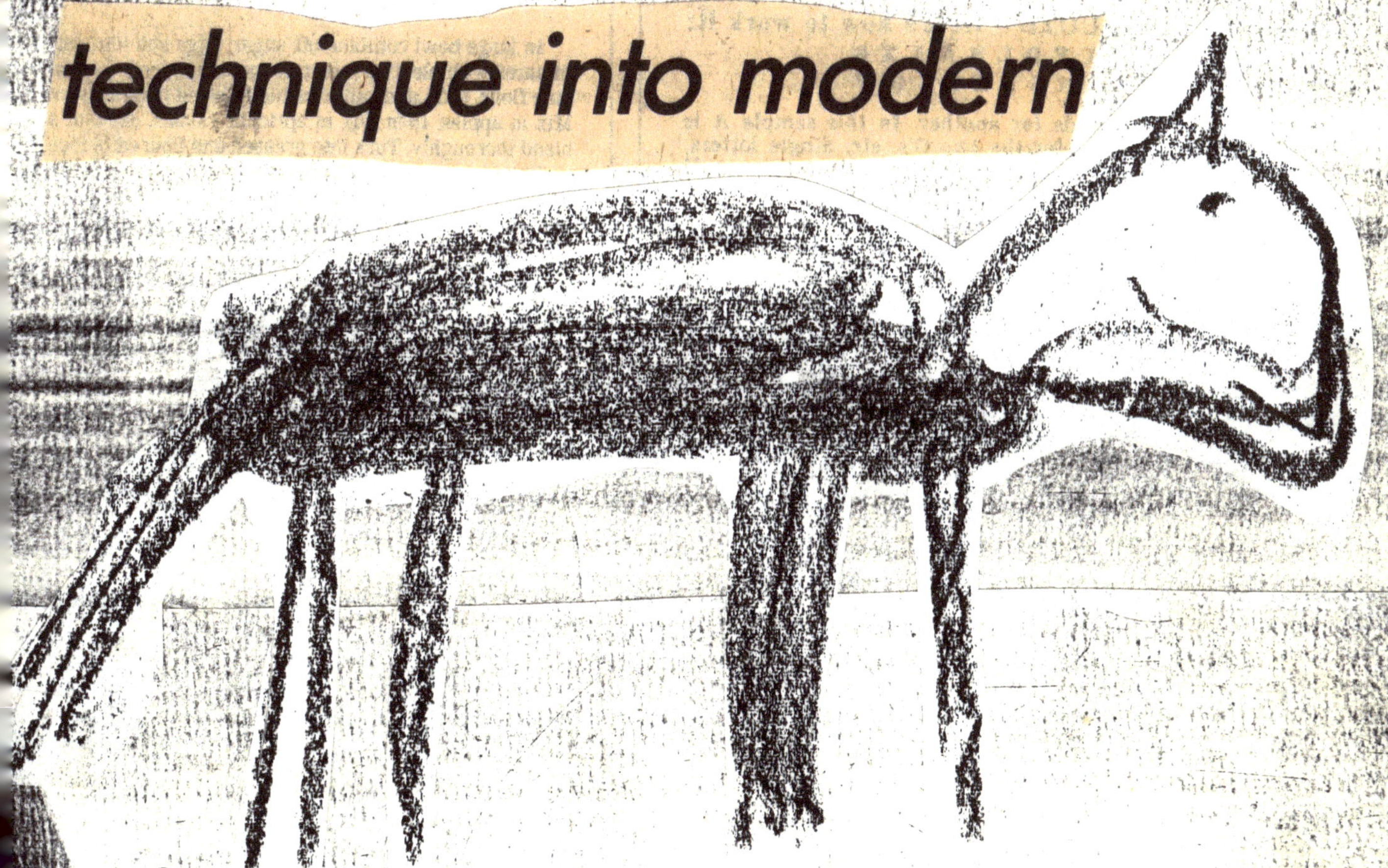

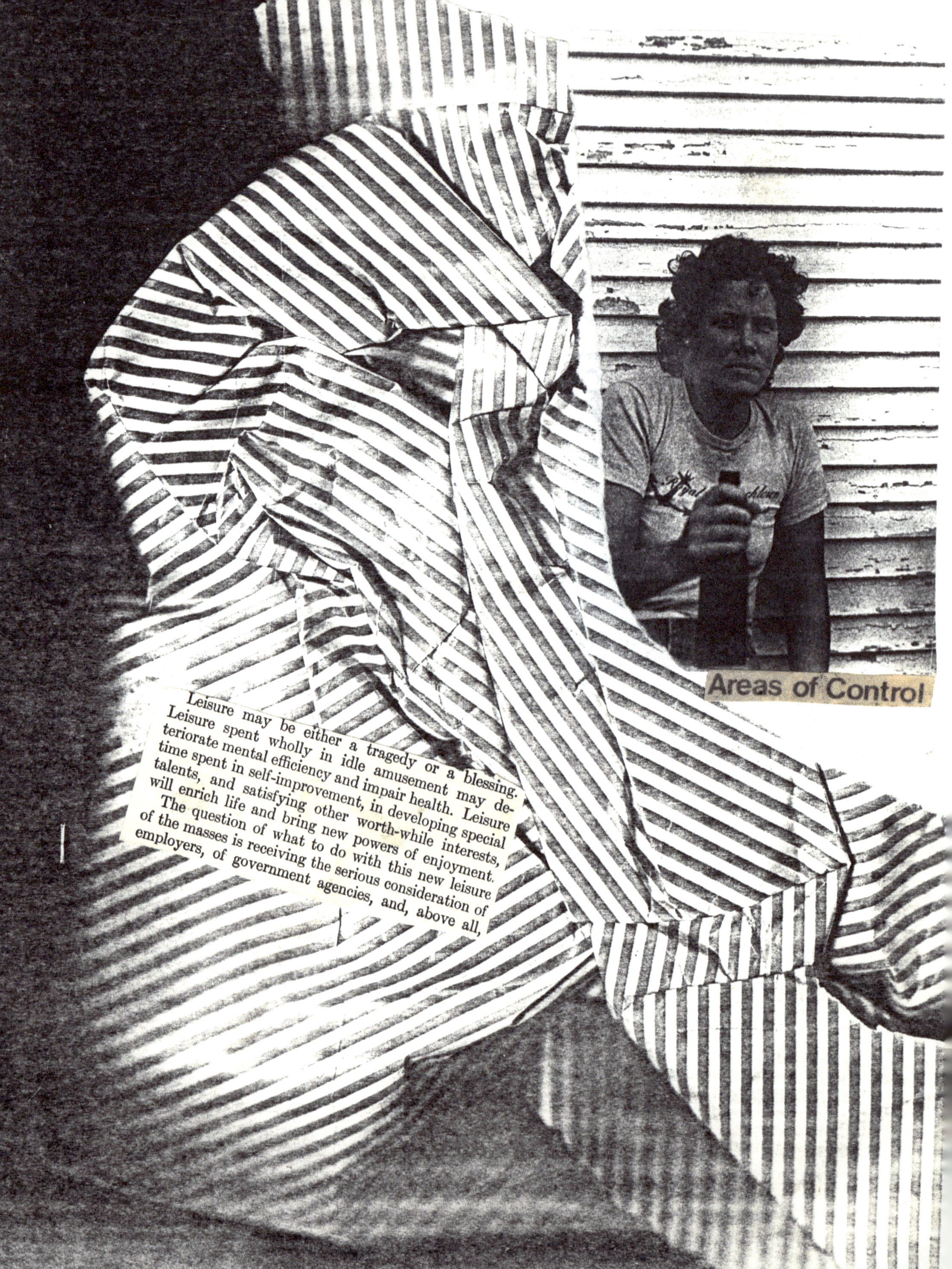
Areas of Control
Leisure may be either a tragedy or a blessing.
Leisure spent wholly in idle amusement may de-
teriorate mental efficiency and impair health. Leisure
time spent in self-improvement, in developing special
talents, and satisfying other worth-while interests,
will enrich life and bring new powers of enjoyment.
The question of what to do with this new leisure
of the masses is receiving the serious consideration of
employers, of government agencies, and, above all,

ARISTOTLE-METAPHYSICS

translated by Richard Hope

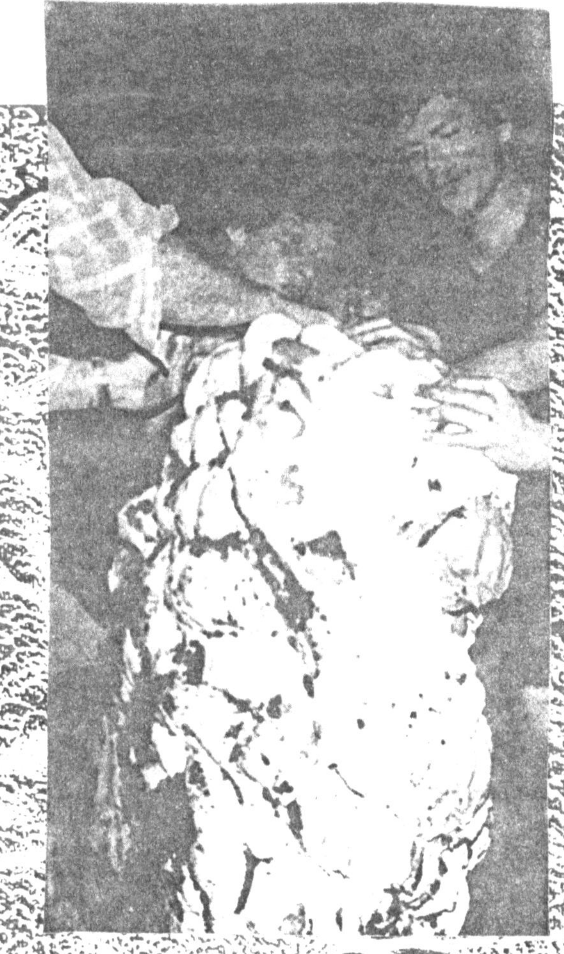

passion dost track
here so far from the track
power breathe
used things all action
upon this sys
through dual holy fashion

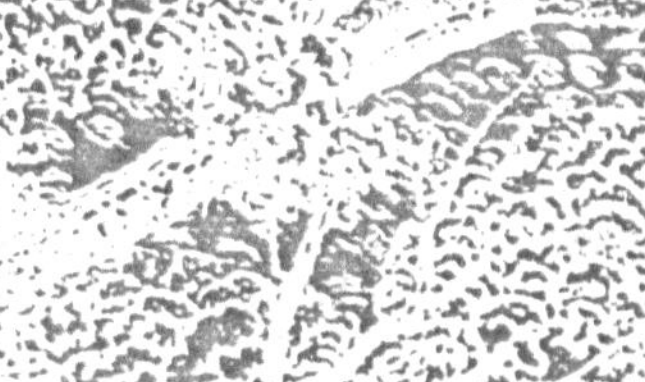

CHART V

AND HERE IT IS.. "THE FLAT CHIN"

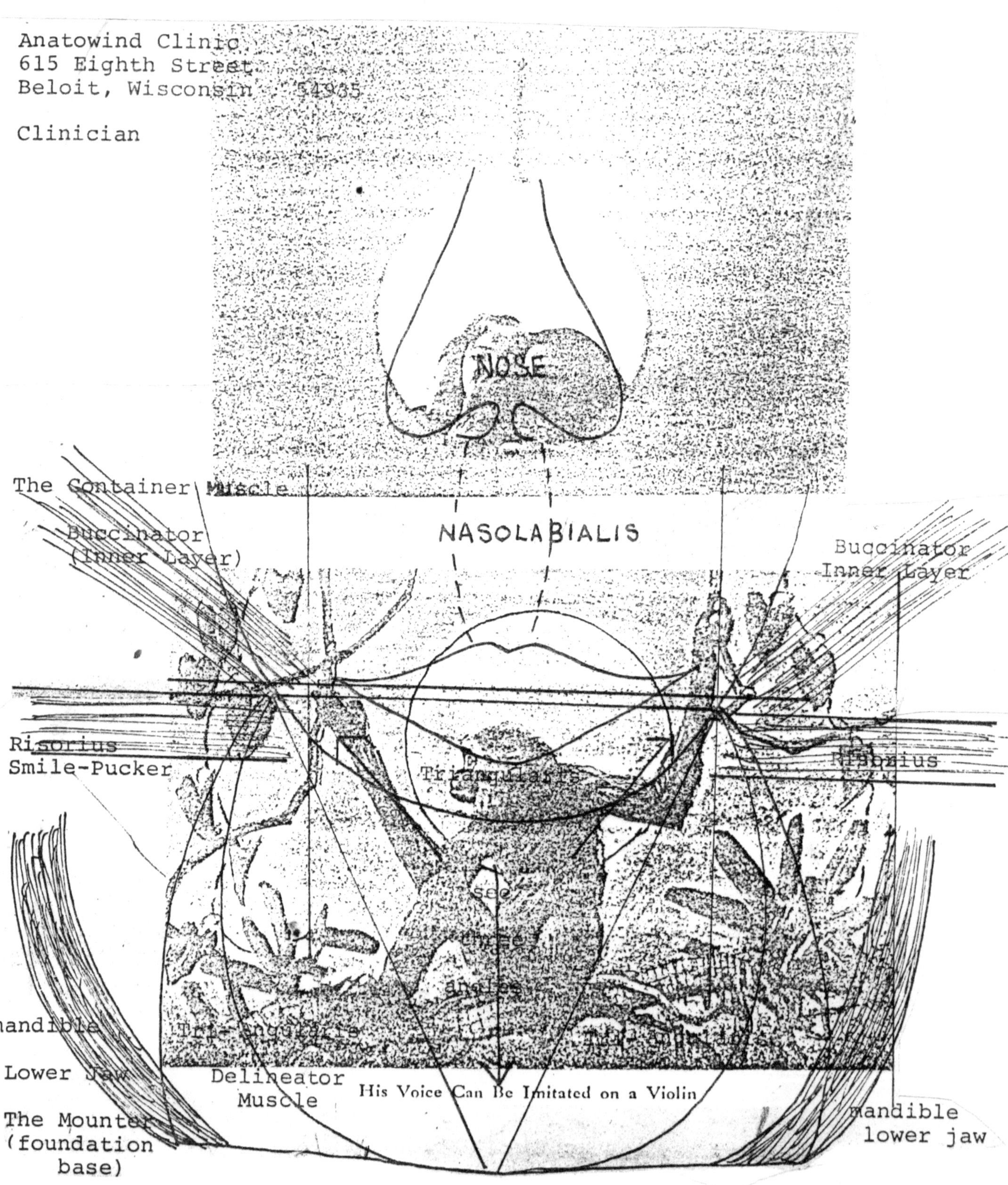

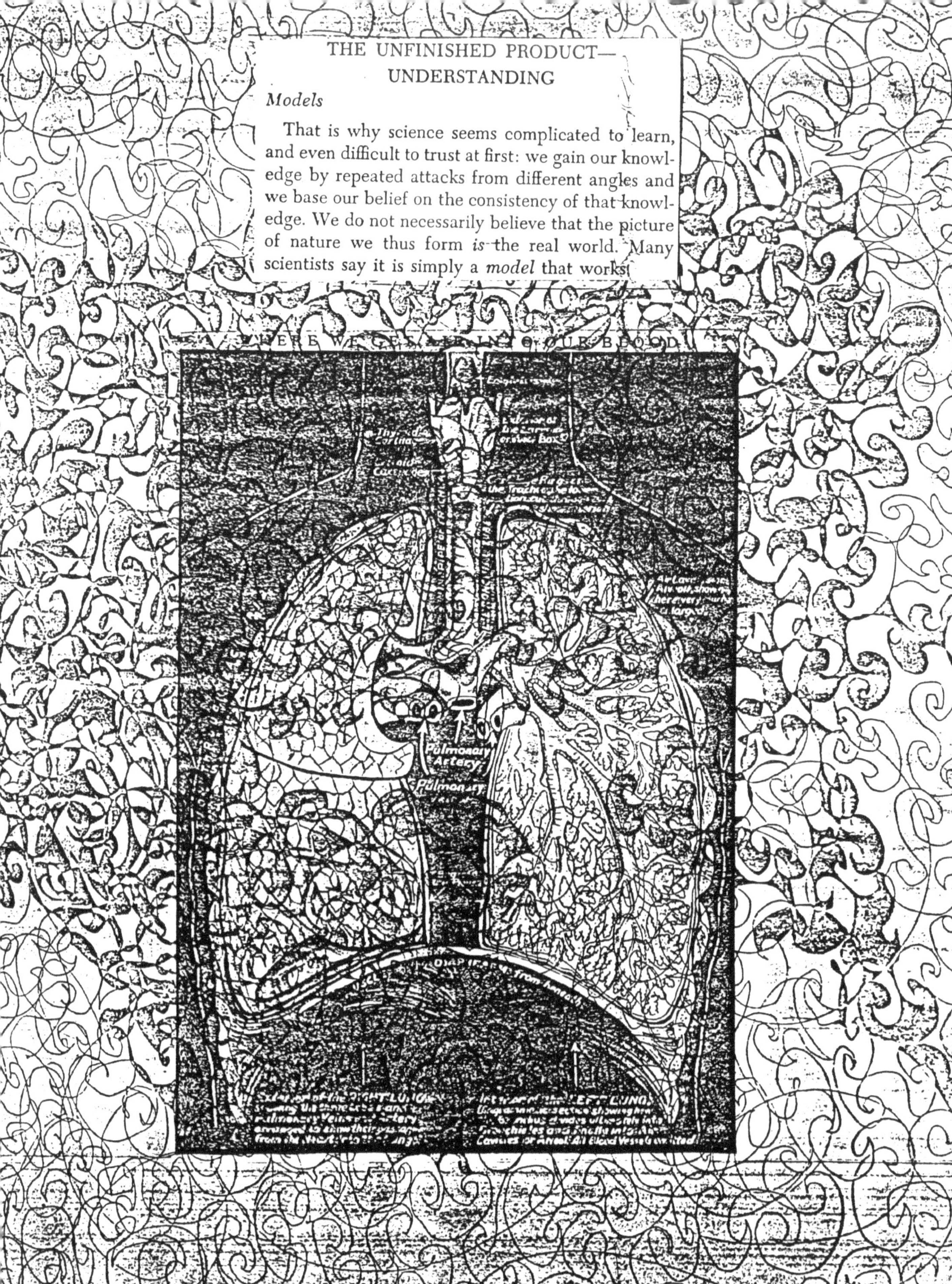

THE UNFINISHED PRODUCT—
UNDERSTANDING

Models

That is why science seems complicated to learn, and even difficult to trust at first: we gain our knowledge by repeated attacks from different angles and we base our belief on the consistency of that knowledge. We do not necessarily believe that the picture of nature we thus form *is* the real world. Many scientists say it is simply a *model* that works.

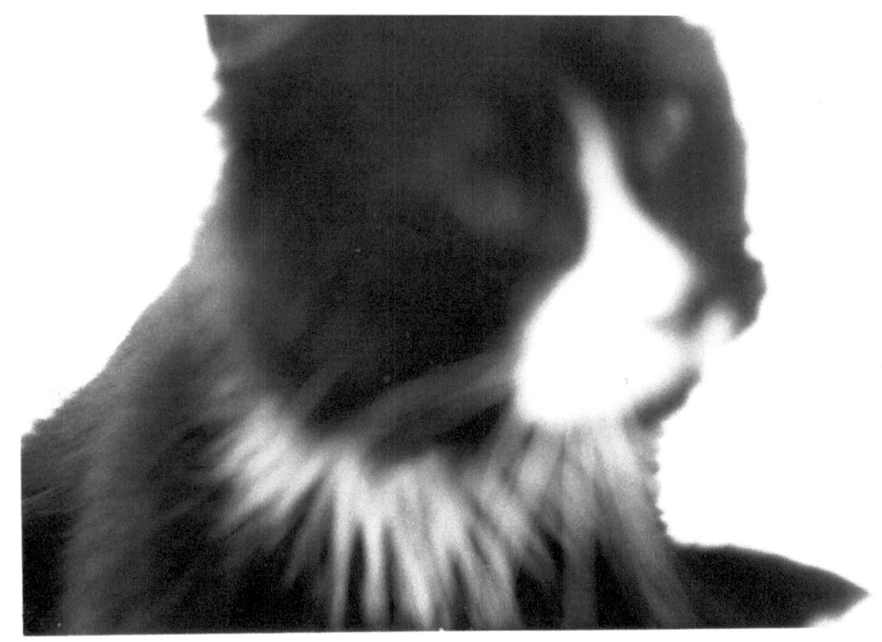

I am a schizophrenic of sorts these days. Living in the air or dying in the mud. Only work is in between scrape scrape paint paint.

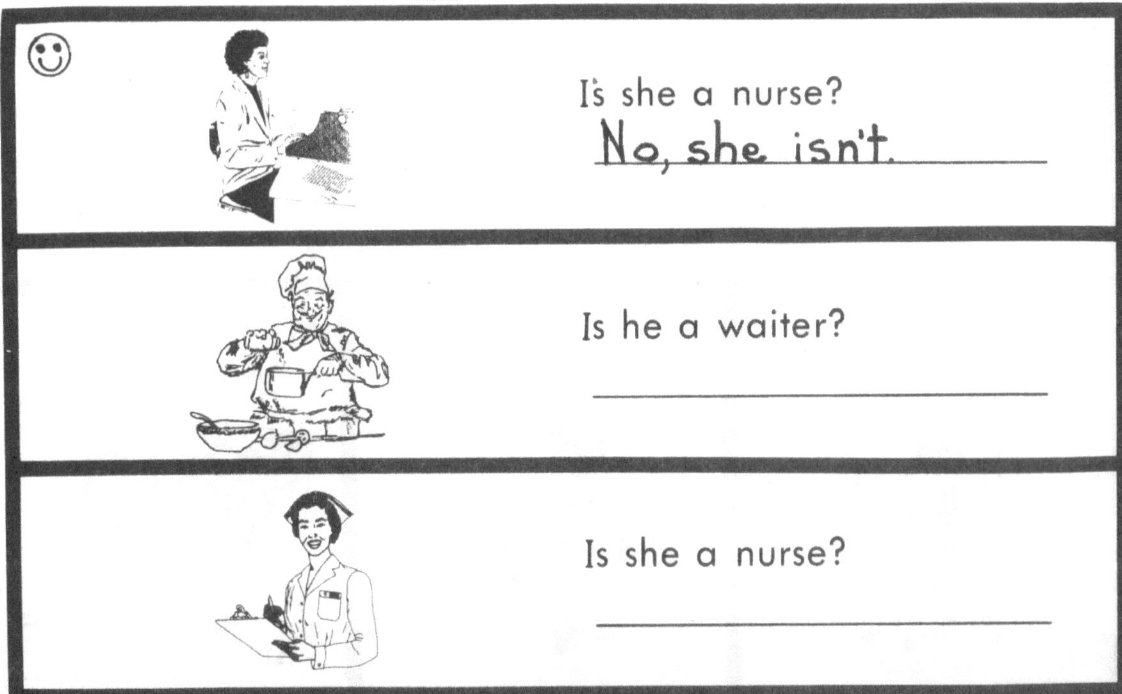

reconcile
belief in
Atheist

and Other Laws of **LEARNING**

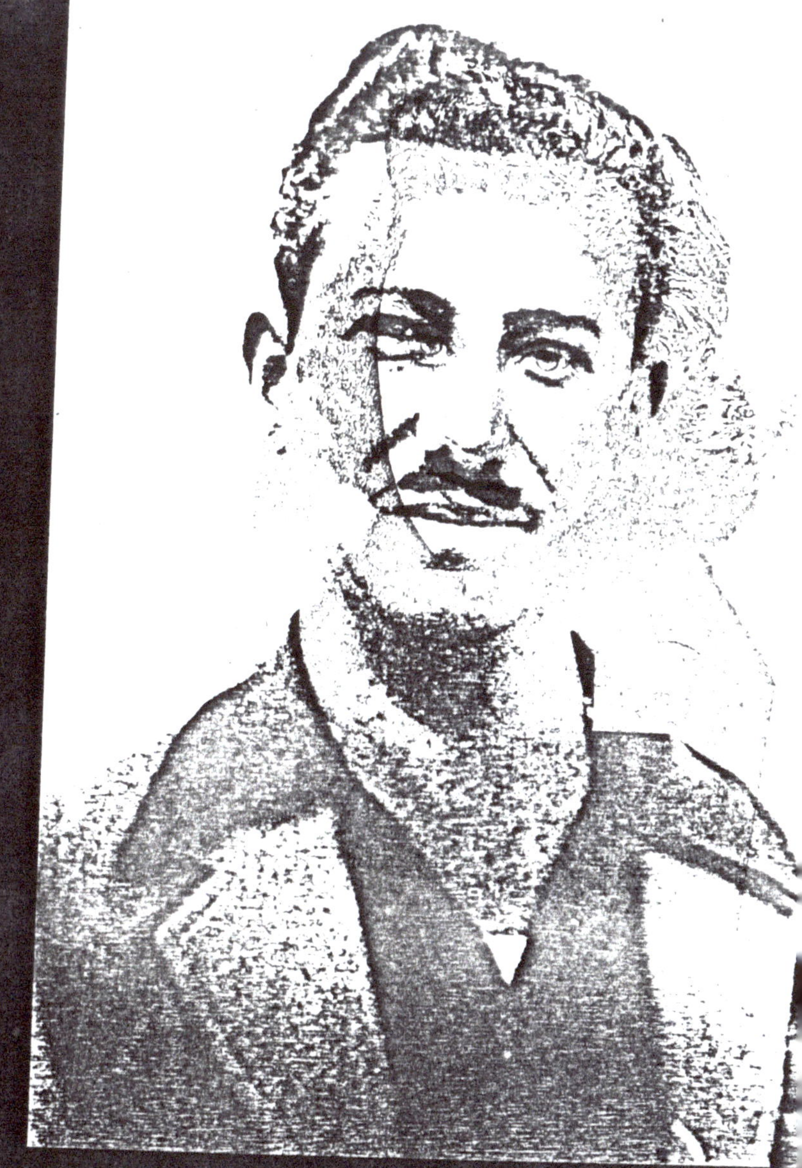

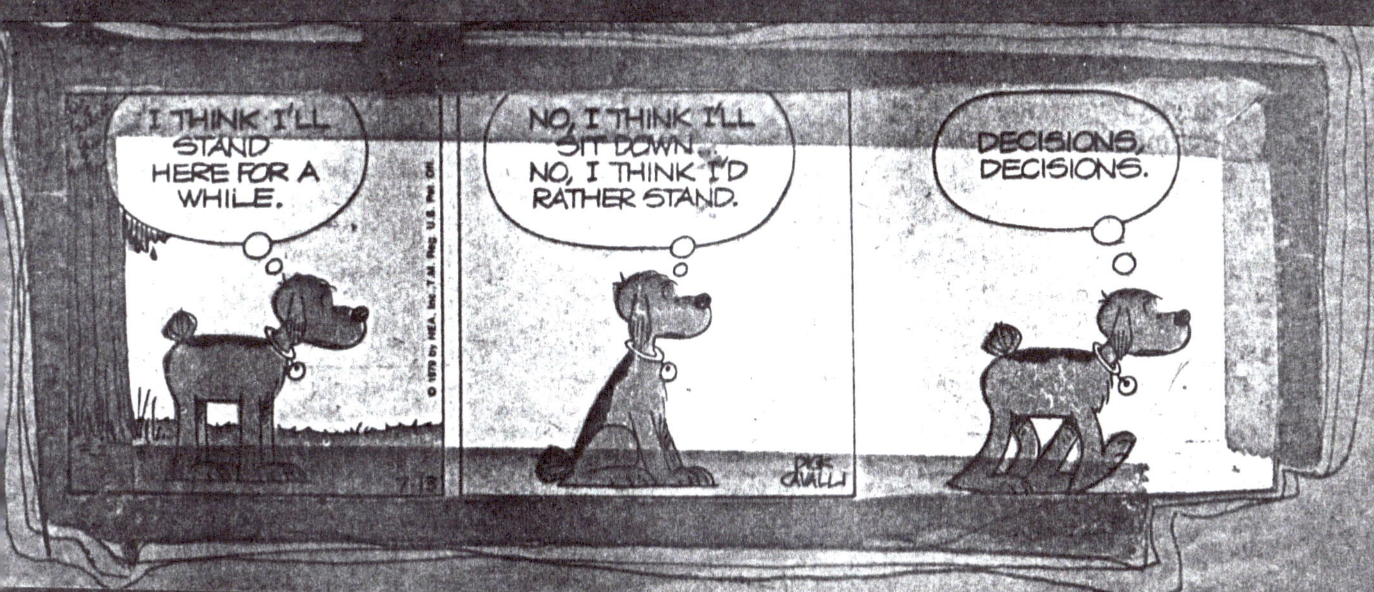

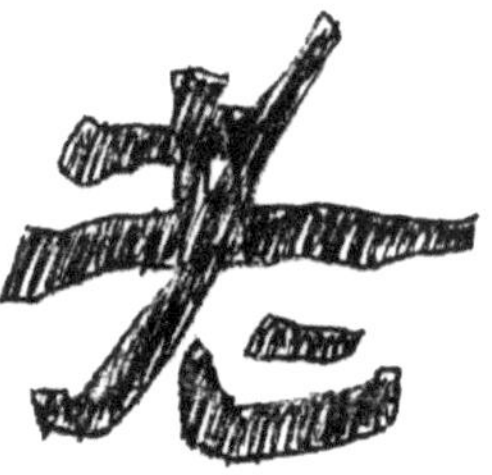

two halve about to come from
below equality joyous and longing
demaned further the table of gains

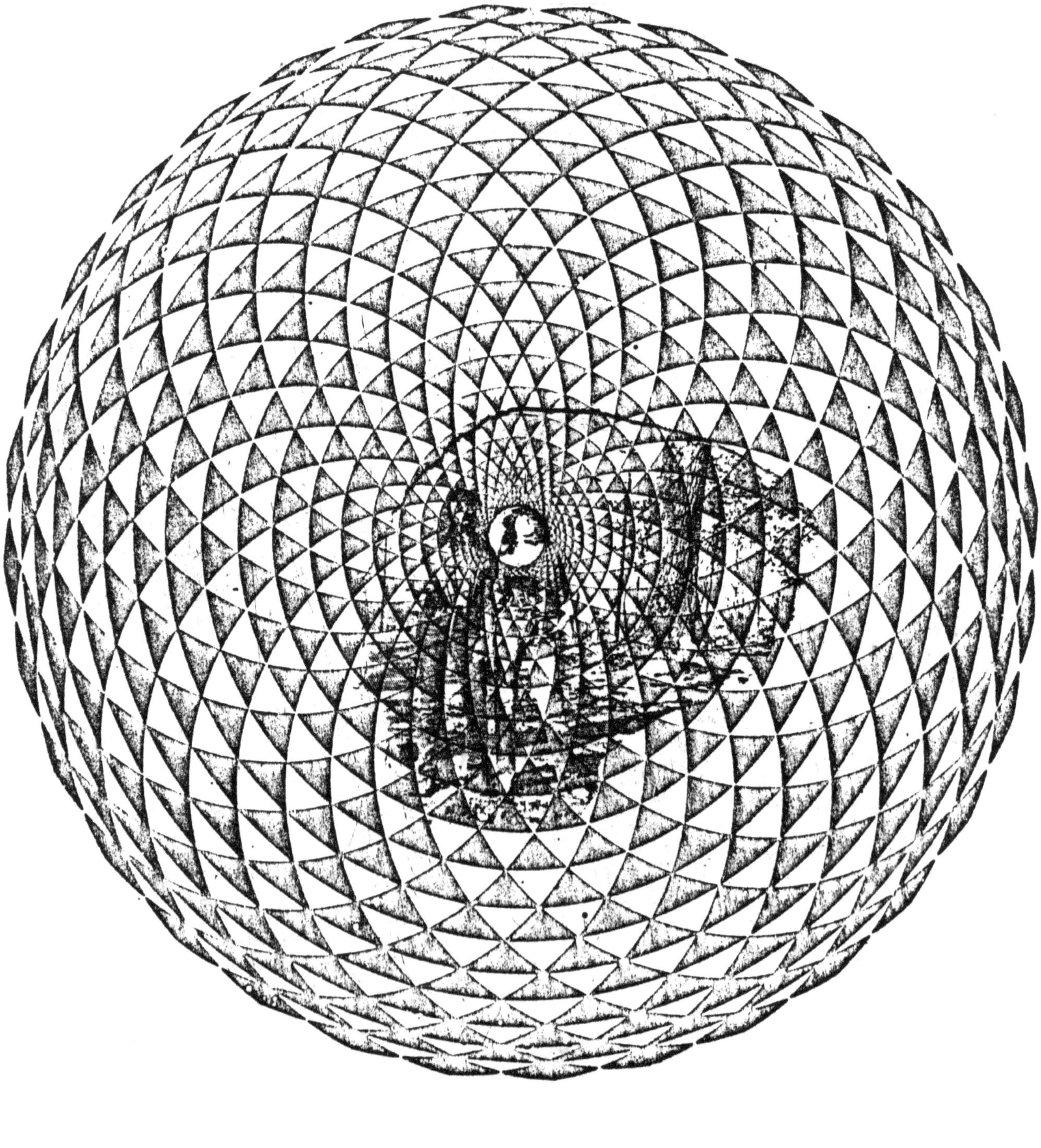

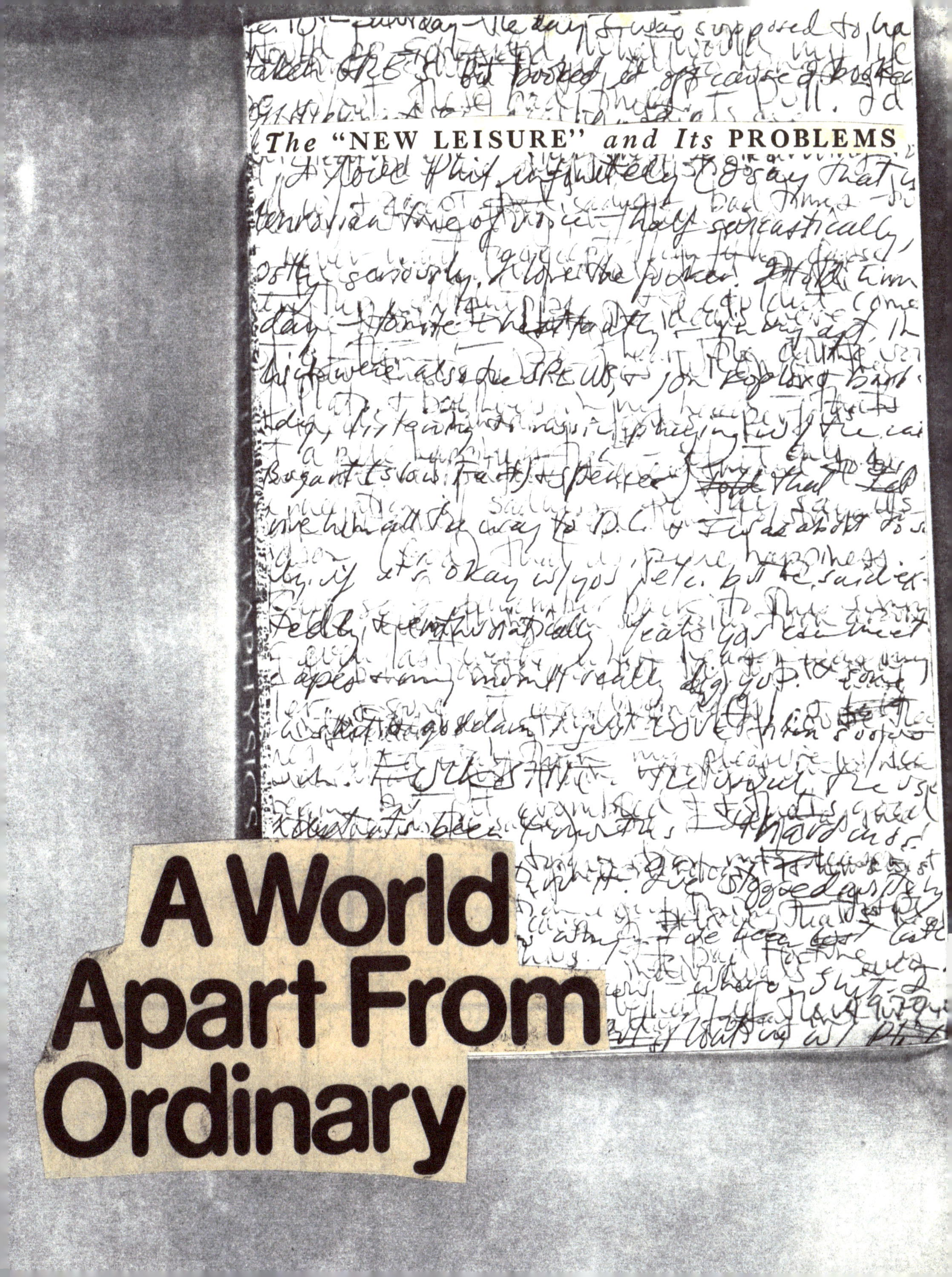

The "NEW LEISURE" and Its PROBLEMS

A World Apart From Ordinary

Dear Schkelez:

Once again, I find myself thinking of your mode. I just finished reading Les Mains Sales, a play by Sartre. I really got into it. The dude can really write. He's the only auth whom I have run into outside of Dostoievsky who can portray people being "ultimately concerned" Tillich would say, with the "eternal questions" without making you want to laugh or puke is, making it seem realistic. The "hero", a typi Sartrian protagoneist, is a member of the landed aristocracy in Illyria (one of the Baltics, I think) ever having had "les mains sales", has a terrible esire to manger de la merde avec les gens. [illegible]

Artist adapts ancient

[illegible] which it portrays... mais qui peut dire quan n joue et quand on ne joue plus? Parce-que t sais, on peut bien jouer à etre serieux. Et tu ré ui, bien joué."

Actually, I've been having a lot of trouble king life seriously recently. I feel as though I s e settling down a bit and making some plans r the FUTURE, but I can't help cracking up henever I envision myself in an established I do find myself however, much more at ease myself, much happier to be me - in my shoes tha ver before. When I think about the future all n I envision is education, this is all that I eally want from life. When I be makin' t most major book of all, I want to be able t y not that I've done this and that and th e been so and so the such and such, but ra at I've seen and known a good chunk of on this planet. When you get down to it,

Up and

over

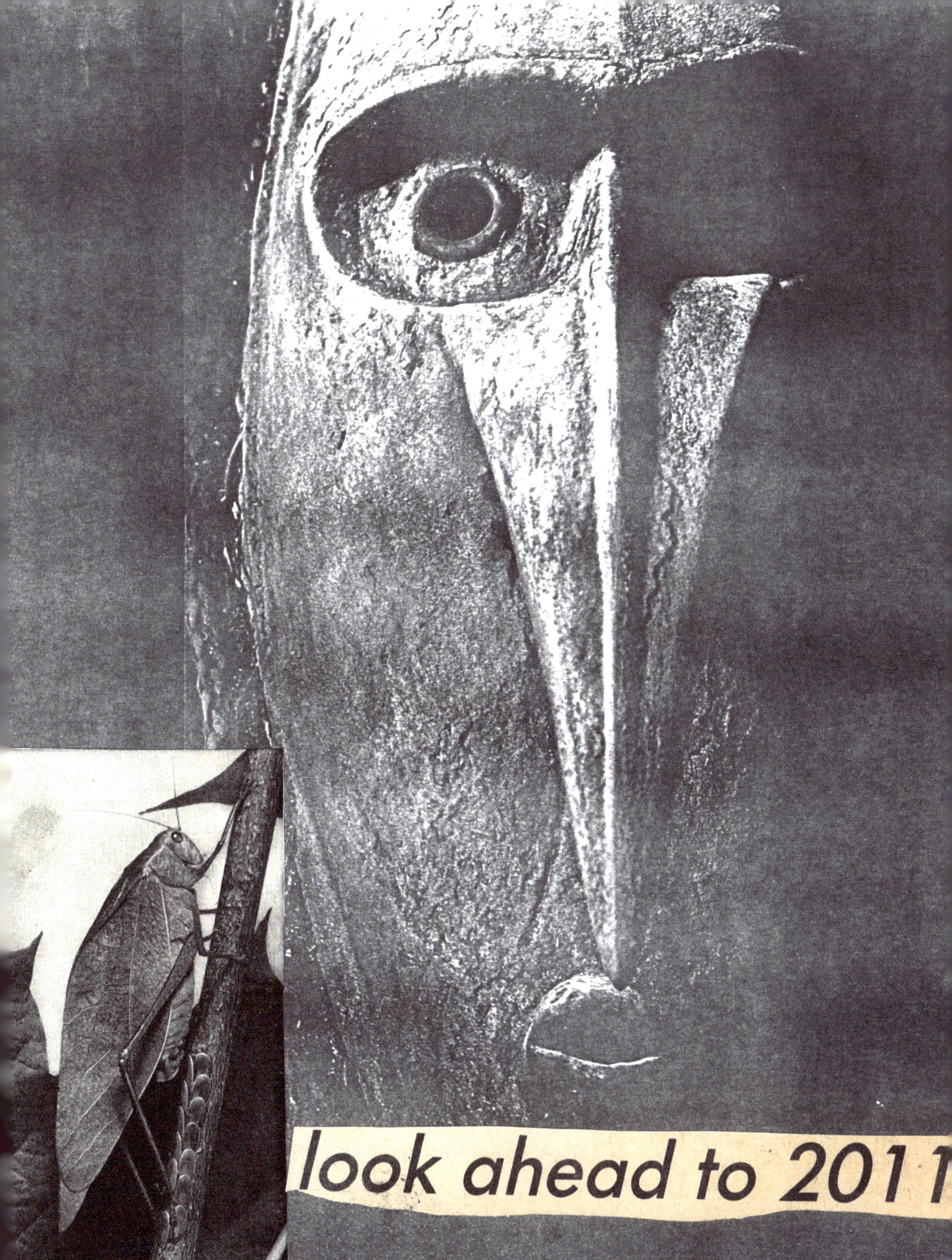
look ahead to 2011

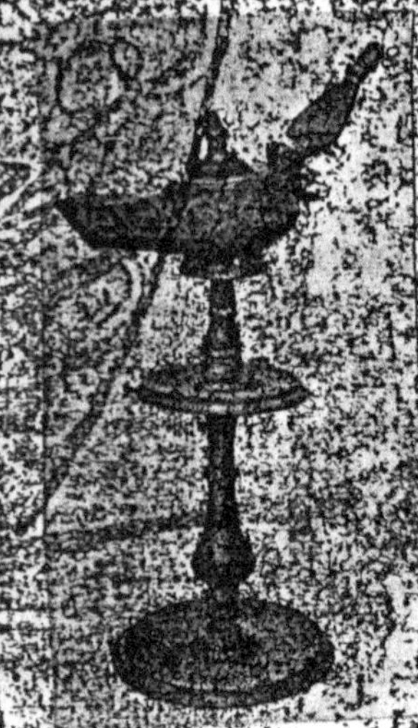

entitled yoga light
matter of my song

AT-
TEN-
TION!

ATTENTION:

Name ______________________ Class ________ Date ________

Title: *Fabric Weaves* Sheet #________

next mission

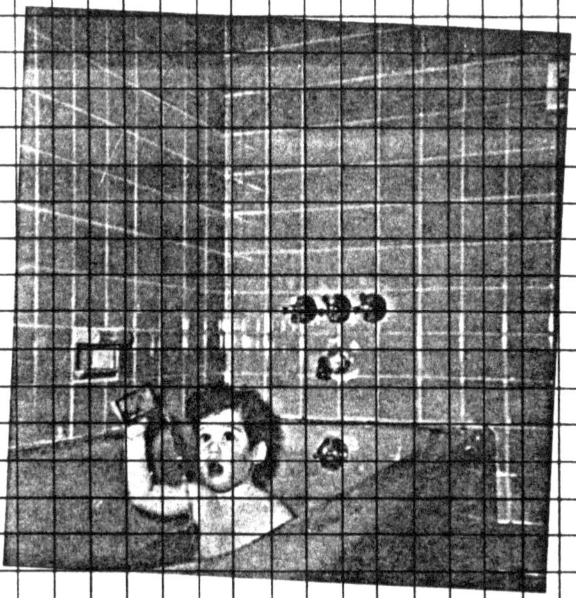

A Social History of Public Schooling in the United States

DAVID NASAW

"Records the remarkably systematic development of American educational institutions, from grade school to university, responsive to a complex and variable set of socio-economic pressures. *Schooled to Order* is . . . . a tribute to the system's sensitivity, if not to its humanity."

Edgar Z. Friedenberg, author of *Coming of Age in America*

What's wrong with our schools?

When radical educators, community activists, and parents first joined forces to demand an answer to this question, the general public's reaction was one of surprise. Now David Nasaw shows that one of the most hotly debated issues of our day is not a new problem.

Schooled to Order lays bare the foundations of the current crisis in public education. Bringing together for the first time an extensive and controversial body of scholarship amassed in the last fifteen years, the book shows that for over a century, the schools have been more interested in teaching poor, immigrant, and minority students their place than in educating them.

The book encompasses the pre-Civil War common school movement, the turn-of-the-century high school reform crusade, and the post-World War II period of college expansion. In each of these periods of reform, public

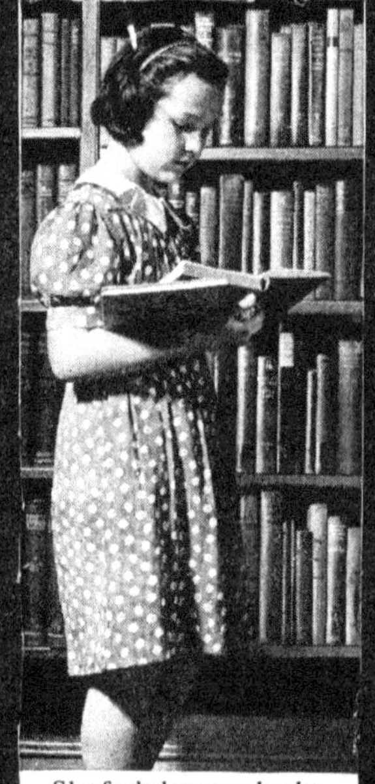

She finds her own books.

"Jonathan Nasaw is a born writer. His technical ease, his generosity and sense of proportion enable him to take what for almost anyone would be an unredeemably grim experience and turn it into a triumph. *Easy Walking* is never grandiose or maudlin—I found it touching, tonic, and very funny."

—Jeremy Larner

EASY WALKING

Jonathan Lewis Nasaw

One dark night twenty-one-year-old Willie Nasaw went for a drive and ran out of road, leaving him with five back vertebrae that, on X-ray film, looked like a pile of crushed sticks. He was paralyzed from the waist down.

For someone else it might have been the end of the road, but not for Willie. Told in his own words, *Easy Walking* is the totally honest and outrageously funny account of Willie's six-month struggle to stand on his own two feet, literally and figuratively.

From the Stryker frame, which flips him over like a fried egg every four hours, to the hydrotherapy tank, where he sinks instead of swims, to simply learning to walk easy in a world that seems to be nothing more than a giant obstacle course—and from bitterness through acceptance to determination—Willie makes an awesome

the flute, returning
arable tabla

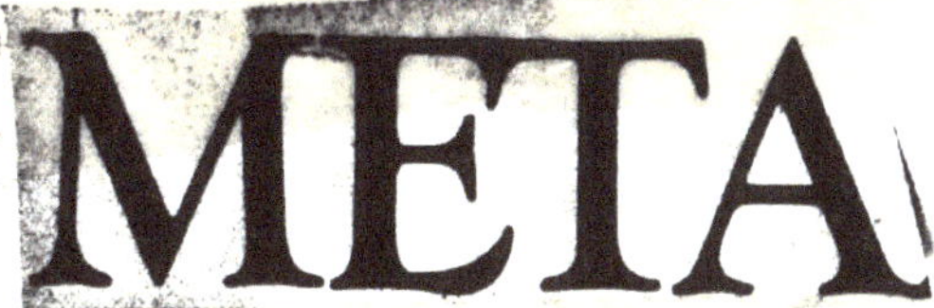

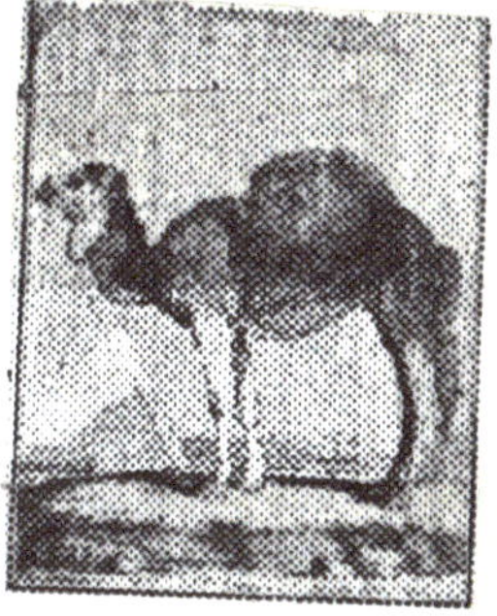

*

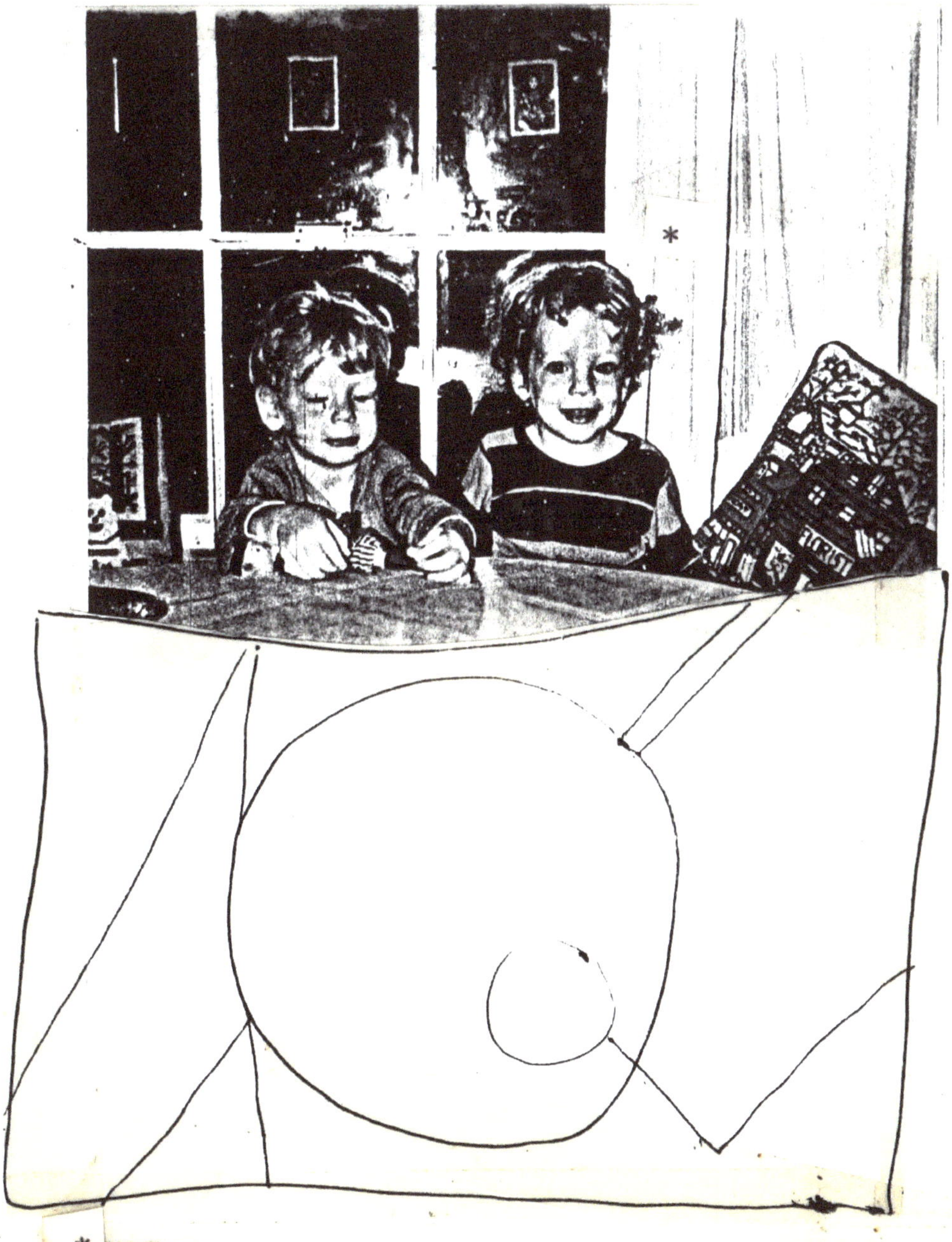

* Experiments in which children are asked to copy geometrical figures have shown that between the ages of three and four they often employ, e.g., two concentric circles to represent a triangle inscribed in a circle.

Index

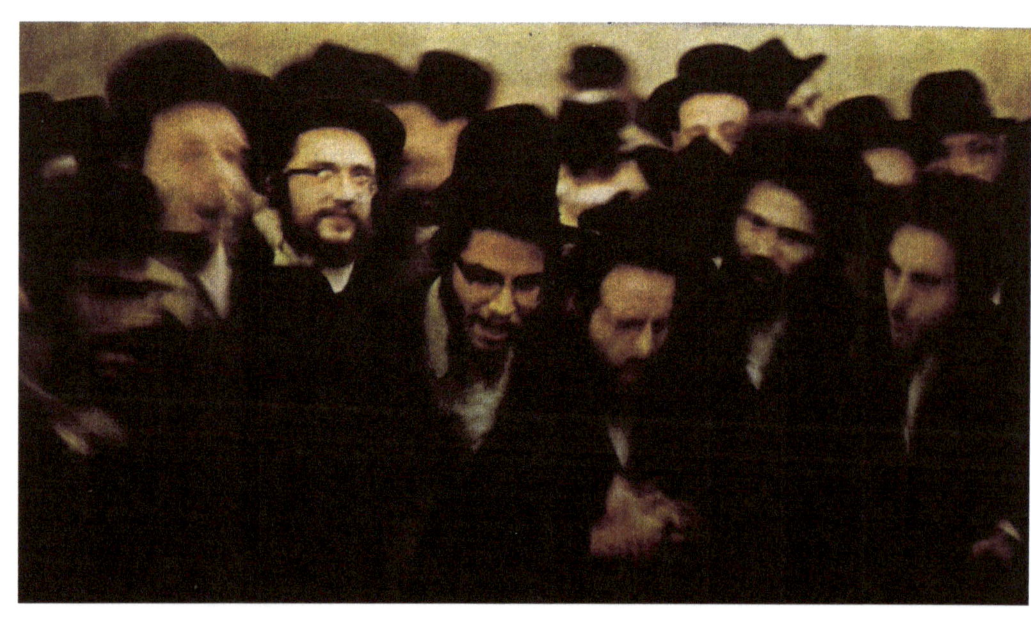

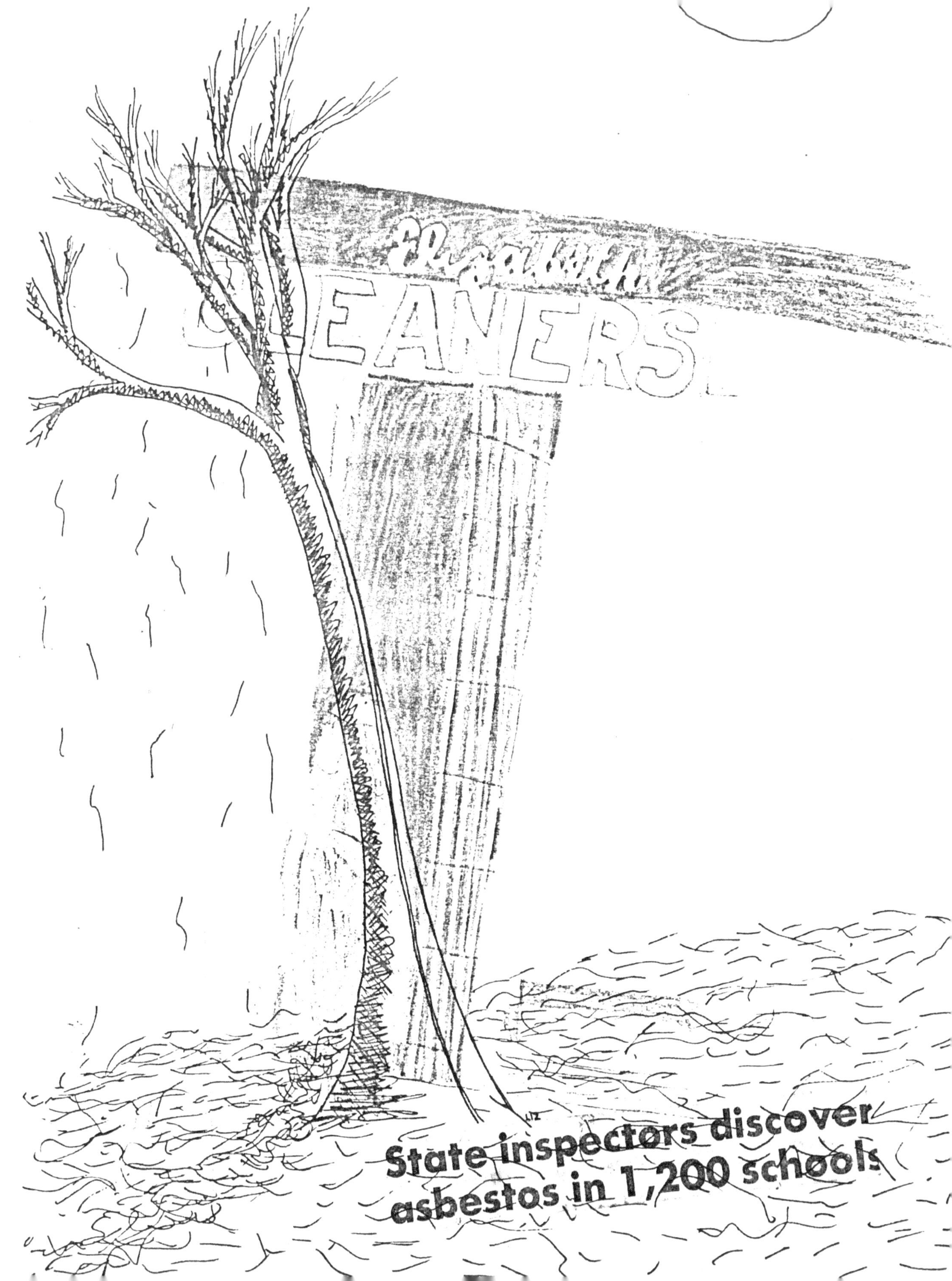
State inspectors discover
asbestos in 1,200 schools

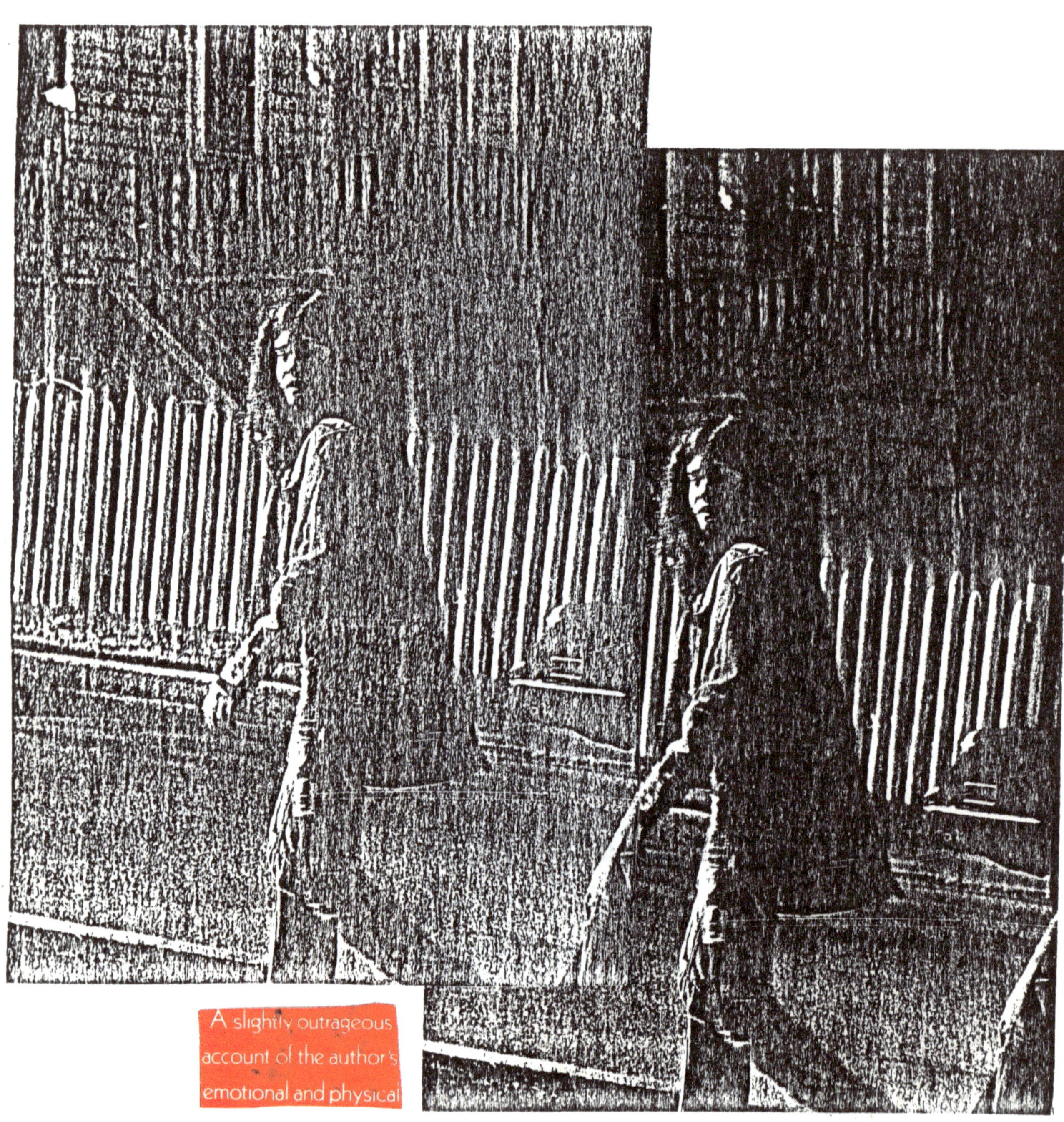

Phrex Brain by Elizabeth Was
Printed in the Autonomous Republic of Qazingulaza

www.ingramcontent.com/pod-product-compliance
Lightning Source LLC
LaVergne TN
LVHW070219110826
845147LV00003B/610

* 9 7 8 1 9 3 6 6 8 7 1 6 9 *